DICTIONARY
of
WORD ROOTS
and
COMBINING FORMS

DICTIONARY
of
WORD ROOTS
and
COMBINING FORMS

Compiled from the Greek, Latin, and other languages,
with special reference to biological terms and scientific names

Donald J. Borror
The Ohio State University

MAYFIELD PUBLISHING COMPANY
Palo Alto, California

First Edition, 1960

Eleventh printing, 1971

Preface

One of the outstanding problems of the biologist, whether he be beginning student or specialist, is that of understanding technical terms. The best way to understand and remember technical terms is to understand first their component parts, or roots. To this end the various word roots, from the Latin, Greek, and other languages, that are most frequently encountered in biological terms have been brought together in this dictionary.

Some of the word roots listed in the following pages are used in many scientific terms and names, and once their meaning is understood their occurrence in words subsequently encountered will immediately suggest the meanings of the new words. The task of looking up a new word in a technical or unabridged dictionary is often eliminated by a knowledge of word roots. The study of the roots of words can become extremely interesting, as well as a very valuable aid in understanding new terms.

This dictionary has been designed primarily to meet the needs of the beginning student, the medical student, and the taxonomist, but it should be of value to all biologists. Both student and teacher are keenly aware of the difficulties of the beginning student in learning technical terms; the medical student is often overwhelmed by the multitude of names of structures, conditions, and processes which he must understand and remember; and the taxonomist frequently encounters words the meanings of which are to be found only in a Latin or Greek dictionary, if at all.

The section on the formulation of scientific names, following the list of word roots, should be of value to the taxonomist who is interested in naming new species or groups.

Table of Contents

How To Use This Dictionary

Every scientific term or name is composed of one or more word roots, between and following which may be one or more vowels or consonants. In the list of roots on the following pages, the connecting vowels and consonants that are most frequently encountered are indicated as variations in the roots. For example, the entry erythr, -o (G) red indicates that the root is erythr and the most commonly encountered connecting vowel is o, and the root may be found as erythr or erythro. The source language of each root is indicated by the abbreviation in parentheses (the root erythr is from a Greek word).

Roots preceded by a hyphen are suffixes, or roots generally used at the end of a word; for example, -idae is the suffix that is added to the roots of generic names to form the names of families of animals, and -pus is the Greek root meaning foot that is used at the end of a word (e.g., octopus). Roots preceded by an equals sign may be used alone or as a terminal root; for example, =buteo, from the Latin and meaning a kind of hawk, is used as Buteo, a genus of hawks; and in the name Archibuteo, another genus of hawks. Root variations preceded by an equals sign are variations usually used at the end of a word; for example, in the entry cephal, =a, -o, the =a indicates that cephala is usually used at the end of a word (as in Acanthocephala, the phylum of spiny-headed worms, parasitic; also a genus of bugs that have a spine on the head).

Similar English meanings are separated by commas, and dissimilar meanings by semicolons. Different English meanings of the same root may be due to the fact that the word from which the root comes has more than one meaning, or the root may be derived from more than one word in the source language; some roots may be derived from words in two source languages, and in such cases the source language is indicated in connection with each English equivalent.

Variations in roots are listed separately in the alphabetical sequence only if they are separated by more than two intervening roots; variations that would be separated by only one or two intervening roots are not repeated in the sequence.

A few examples will serve to illustrate the use of this dictionary.

1

<u>Micromere</u>. In the following pages will be found:

micr, -o (G) small
mer, =e, -i, -o (G) a part; the thigh
  In this case the variations are <u>mer</u>, <u>-mere</u>, <u>meri</u>, and
  <u>mero</u>; the =e indicates that <u>mere</u> is usually used at the end of
  a term or name. The two English equivalents here are the re-
  sult of the root coming from two Greek words.
-mere (G) a part
  The hyphen before the root indicates that it is usually used
  at the end of a term or name.

The first part of the word <u>micromere</u> means small; the last part
means a part; a micromere is thus a small part of something.

<u>Osmoderma eremicola</u> (the scientific name of the hermit flower
beetle). In the following pages will be found:

osm, =a, -i, -o (G) a smell, odor
osmo, -s, -t (G) pushing, thrusting
derm, =a, -ato, -o (G) skin
erem, -i, -o (G) lonely, solitary
col, (L) with, together; (G) colon; limb
col, -a, -i (L) dwell

The <u>osmo</u> part of the genus name might come from either of the
two roots listed but, since this beetle has a rather distinct odor, it
would appear that the first of the two roots (meaning smell or odor)
is the one used; <u>derma</u> means skin. The genus name therefore refers
to the characteristic odor of this insect. The first part of the species
name means lonely or solitary; since <u>cola</u> is indicated as a variation
in the root meaning to dwell, this root is evidently the one used; the
species name thus means living alone (or as a hermit, hence the
common name of the insect).

<u>Pododynia</u>. In the following pages will be found:

pod, -o, =y (G) a foot
odyn, =e, =ia, -o (G) pain
dyn, -am, -amo, -ast (G) be able; power, energy

The first part of the word <u>pododynia</u> obviously comes from a Greek word meaning foot. Since the first of the other two roots (odyn) indicates ia as terminating vowels, this is obviously the root involved. Podo is the form of this root usually used, but since it is followed by another root beginning with o, the final o of podo is omitted. Pododynia thus means pain in the foot.

ABBREVIATIONS

Af - African	LL - Low Latin; Late Latin
Ar - Arabic	Mal - Malayan
AS - Anglo-Saxon	Mex - Mexican
Br - Brazilian	ME - Middle English
Ch - Chilean	ML - Middle Latin
Dan - Danish	My - Mythology
E - English	N - a proper name
EI - East Indian	NL - New Latin
F - French	OF - Old French
Far - Faroese	OHG - Old High German
G - Greek	Pg - Portuguese
Ger - German	Pp - Papuan
Go - Gothlandic	Ps - Persian
H - Hindustani	Pv - Peruvian
Hb - Hebrew	Rs - Russian
Ice - Icelandic	SAm - South American
It - Italian	Sp - Spanish
L - Latin	Sw - Swedish

RULES FOR PRONUNCIATION OF
SCIENTIFIC NAMES

Vowels. All vowels in scientific names are pronounced. Vowels are generally either long or short, and in the examples which follow a long vowel sound is indicated by a grave accent (`), and short vowels by an acute accent (´); e.g., màte, mát, mète, mét, bìte, bít, ròpe, rót, cùte, cút, bỳ, sýmmetry. A vowel at the end of a word has the long sound, except when it is a; a final a has an uh sound, as in idea. The vowel in the final syllable of a word has the short sound, except es, which is pronounced ease.

Diphthongs. A diphthong consists of two vowels written together and pronounced as a single vowel. The diphthongs are ae (pronounced ē), oe (usually pronounced ē, rarely ē), oi (pronounced as in oil), eu (pronounced ū), ei (pronounced ī), ai (pronounced ā), and au (pronounced as in August).

Consonants. Ch has the k sound, except in words derived from a language other than Greek. When c is followed by ae, e, oe, i, or y, it has the soft (s) sound; when it is followed by a, o, oi, or u, it has the hard (k) sound. When g is followed by ae, e, i, oe, or y, it has the soft (j) sound; when it is followed by a, o, oi, or u, it has the hard sound (as in go). In words beginning with ps, pt, ct, cn, gn, or mn, the initial letter is not pronounced, but when these letters appear together in the middle of a word the first letter is pronounced. An x at the beginning of a word is pronounced as z, but as ks when it appears elsewhere in a word. When a double c is followed by i or y, it is pronounced as ks.

Accent. The accented syllable is either the penult or the antepenult (in very long words there may be a secondary accent on a syllable near the beginning of the word). The principal rules governing the syllable accented and the vowel sound (whether long or short) are as follows:

1. The accent is on the penult syllable in the following cases:

   a. When the word contains only two syllables. Ex.: Àpis, Úlmus.

   b. When the penult contains a diphthong. Ex.: Hemileùca, Lygaèus, Nymphaèa, Spiraèa.

   c. When the vowel in the penult is followed by x or z. Ex.: Agromỹza, Melospìza, Coríxa, Lespedèza, Prodōxus.

   d. When the vowel in the penult is long. Whether this vowel is long or short often depends on the derivation of the word and the vowel sound in the source language. For example, in words derived from the Greek μηρὸς, meaning thigh, the e is long (ex.: epimèron, Diapheromèra); while in those derived from μεμρος, meaning part, the e is short (ex.: Heterómera). The penult vowel is usually long in the following cases:

      1) Words derived from Latin past participles and ending in -ata, -atus, or -atum. Ex.: maculàta. (The penult vowel

is short in such Greek plurals as <u>Echinodérmata</u>.)

2) Latin adjectives ending in -alis. Ex.: <u>orientàlis</u>, <u>verticàlis</u>, <u>lateràlis</u>.

3) Words ending in <u>-ina</u>. Ex.: <u>Spartìna</u>, <u>Glossìna</u>, <u>Hetaerìna</u>.

4) Words ending in <u>-ica</u>. Ex.: <u>Formìca</u>, <u>Melìca</u>, <u>Myrmìca</u>, <u>Fulìca</u>.

5) Words ending in <u>-ana</u>, <u>-anus</u>, or <u>-anum</u>. Ex.: <u>Tabànus</u>, <u>Porzàna</u>, <u>mexicànum</u>.

6) Words ending in <u>-ura</u>. Ex.: <u>Thysanùra</u>, <u>Xiphosùra</u>, <u>Chaetùra</u>.

7) Words ending in <u>-odes</u> or <u>-otes</u>. Ex.: <u>Sabulòdes</u>, <u>Sphecòdes</u>, <u>Hylòdes</u>, <u>Epiròtes</u>.

8) Words ending in <u>-ates</u>. Ex.: <u>Aceràtes</u>, <u>Dryobàtes</u>, <u>Hippelàtes</u>.

9) Words ending in <u>-ales</u>. Ex.: the names of plant orders, e.g., <u>Graminàles</u>.

10) Words ending in <u>-inae</u>. Ex.: the names of animal subfamilies, e.g., <u>Papilionìnae</u>.

11) Words ending in <u>-osis</u>. Ex.: <u>pediculòsis</u>, <u>trichinosis</u>; there are a few exceptions in modern usage, e.g., <u>metamórphosis</u>.

12) Words ending in <u>-soma</u>. Ex.: <u>Calosòma</u>, <u>Eriosòma</u>.

13) Words ending in <u>-pogon</u>. Ex.: <u>Andropògon</u>, <u>Calopògon</u>.

14) Words ending in <u>-chlora</u>. Ex.: <u>Augochlòra</u>.

15) Words in which the vowel of the penult is <u>u</u>, except when the <u>u</u> is followed by <u>l</u>. Ex.: <u>Fenùsa</u>, <u>Ctenùcha</u>, <u>Sambùcus</u>. Exceptions: <u>Libéllula</u>, <u>Bétula</u>, <u>Campánula</u>, <u>Sanícula</u>.

16) When the vowel is followed by <u>z</u>. Ex.: <u>Agromỳza</u>, <u>Triòza</u>, <u>Lespedèza</u>, <u>Ophiorrhìza</u>.

e. When the vowel of the penult is short and followed by two consonants, except a mute followed by <u>l</u> or <u>r</u>. Ex.: <u>Pseudocóccus</u>, <u>Chlorélla</u>, <u>Caulophýllum</u>, <u>Vanéssa</u>, <u>Chlorotéttix</u>, <u>Coreópsis</u>, <u>Latrodéctus</u>, <u>Lithospérmum</u>, <u>Eriánthus</u>, <u>Agróstis</u>, <u>Gryllotálpa</u>,

Rhododéndron, Derméstes, Pyromórpha, Cordulegáster. When the vowel of the penult is followed by a mute (b, hard c, d, g, k, p, q, t, ch, ph, or th) and l or r, the accent is on the antepenult; ex.: Geómetra, Ánabrus, Ránatra, Melánoplus, Rhombólytrum, Stenóbothrus.

2. In other cases the accent is on the antepenult.

  a. The vowel of the antepenult is long in the following cases:

   1) When it is followed by another vowel. Ex.: Epèolus, Sìalis, Rhodìola, Hepìalus, Pìeris. This includes the names of animal families which have a vowel immediately preceding the -idae; ex.: Danàidae, Trupanèidae, Gavìidae, Melòidae, Grùidae, Stratiomỳidae.

   2) When it is a, e, o, or u, followed by a single consonant and two vowels, the first of which is e, i, or y. Ex.: Aràneus, Gerànium, Castànea, Phacèlia, Tèlea, Orthèzia, Nemòbius, Numènius, Pogònia, Pìcea, Siàlia, Lànius, Conopòdium. This is the case in the names of plant families (e g., Malvàceae).

   3) When it is u and followed by a single consonant. Ex.: Linguatùlida, Redùvius, Cordùlia, pellùcidus.

   4) When it is a diphthong. Ex.: Clathronèuria, Linotaènia.

  b. The vowel of the antepenult is short in other cases. This includes all animal family names in which the antepenult is followed by a consonant (except when the vowel is u); ex.: Anátidae, Trypétidae, Mímidae, Chrysópidae, Agromýzidae. The following names, and others with similar endings, have the antepenult vowel short: Heterócera, Geócoris, Conocéphalus, Troglódytes, Empídonax, Chauliógnathus, Pantógrapha, Chirónomus, Mallóphaga, Orthóptera, Micrópteryx, Chilópoda, Triátoma, Neuróspora, Drosóphila, Trichómonas, Melanóstoma.

Dictionary of Word Roots and
Combining Forms

A

a (G). Not, without; together
aapt, -o (G). Unapproachable, invincible
ab, -s (L). Off, from, away
abact (L). Driven away
abbreviat (L). Shortened
abdicat (L). Disinherit
abdit (L). Secret, hidden
abdom, =en, -in (L). The abdomen
aberran (L). Going astray
abie, =s, -t (L). A fir tree
abject (L). Downcast, spiritless
ablat (L). Weaned, removed
ablep, -s (G). Blindness
ablut (L). Washed, cleansed
abort, -iv (L). Born prematurely
abr, -o (G). Delicate, dainty, pretty
=abramis (G). A kind of fish
abras (L). Rubbed off, scraped off
abrot (G). Not edible; divine; splendor
abroton (G). A kind of plant
abrupt (L). Broken away from, steep
abs (L). Off, from, away
abscis, -s (L). Cut off
absinth, =ium (L). Wormwood
absit (L). Distant
abstemi (L). Temperate, moderate
abund (L). Overflow
abyss, -o (G). Deep, bottomless
ac (L). To, toward
aca (G). A point; silence; healing

acalanth, -i, =is (G). A goldfinch
acaleph, =a (G). A nettle
acanth, =a, -o (G). A spine, thorn
acanthi, -d, =s (G). A goldfinch
acar, -in (G). A kind of mite; tiny
acceler (L). Hasten
accip (L). Seize, accept
=accipiter (L). A hawk
accliv (L). Steep, up-hill
accresc (L). Increase
ace, -o (G). Heal; remedy
-aceae (the ending of plant family names)
=acer (L). Sharp; a maple tree
acerb (L). Bitter, sour
acerv, =us (L). A heap
acest (G). Healing; remedy
acestr, =a (G). A darning needle
acet, -o, =um, =yl (L). Vinegar
acetabul, =um (L). A vinegar cup
ach (G). Ache, pain
achen (G). Poor, needy; not gaping
achet, =a, -o (L). Singing, sounding; a cicada
achille (G My). A character who had a vulnerable heel
achly, -o, =s (G). Gloom, darkness
achn, =a (G). Chaff, froth
achr, -oio, -oo, -ost (G). Colorless
achth, -o, =us (G). A weight, burden
achyr, -o, =um (G). Chaff, bran
aci, -do, =us (G). A point, barb
acicul, =a (L). A small needle
acid (L). Sour, sharp
acin, -i, -o, =us (L). A berry
acinac, =es (L). A short sword

7

-acious (E). Abounding in
=acipenser (L). The sturgeon
=acis (G). A point, barb
acli, -d, =s (L). A small javelin
acm, =a (G). The highest point;
  a point
acmae, -o (G). Flourishing, mature
=acmon, -o (G). An anvil
aco (G). A cure, remedy, relief
acoet, =es (G). A bedfellow, spouse
acoluth, -o (G). Following
aconit, =um (L). The monk's-hood
acont, -i, =um, -o (G). A javelin,
  dart
acost, =a (G). Barley
acous, -t (G). Hear; heard
acr, =a, -e (G). At the apex
acr, -i (L). Sharp
acri, -d, =s (G). A locust
acrib, -o (G). Exact
acrit, -o (G). Confused
acro (G). Topmost, the tip
acromi, -o, =um (G). The point of
  the shoulder blade
act, =a, -e, -i (G). The beach, seashore
acti, -no, =s (G). A ray, beam
actit, =es (G). A shore dweller
actuos (L). Lively, active
acu, =s (L). A needle
acu, -st (G). Hear; heard
acule, =us (L). A sting, thorn
acumin, -a (L). A point; pointed
=acus (L). A needle
=acus (G). A cure, remedy, relief
acust (G). Hear; heard
acut (L). Sharp
ad (L). To, toward
adama, -nto (G). Unconquerable;
  diamond; iron
adapi (NL). A rabbit
addict (L). Devoted, compelled

ade (G). Enough, abundantly; to be
  sated
adelo (G). Unknown, secret
adelph, =us (G). Brother
=aden, -o (G). A gland
adephag, -o (G). Gluttonous
=adeps, adip, -o (L). Fat
adminicul, =or (L). A support, prop
adnex (L). Bound to, annexed
adol, -o (G). Genuine, pure
adolesc (L). Growing up
adore, =us (L). Grain, spelt
adox, -o (G). Insignificant; disrep-
  utable
adr, -o (G). thick, stout
adran (G). Feeble, listless
adras (L). Shaved, scraped away
adul, -a (L). Flatter
adulter (L). Corrupt, pollute
adust (L). Burned, tanned
ae (see also ai, e, or oe)
aechm, =a, -o (G). A spear
aeci, =a, -di (G). An injury
aed, =es, -i (L). A temple; a dwelling
aedeag (NL). The genitals
=aedes (G). Disagreeable
aedoe, -o (G). Regard with reverence;
  the genitals
=aedon (G). A nightingale
aeger, -i (L My). A nymph
aegi, -di, =s (L). A shield
aegial, -o, =us (G). The seashore,
  beach
aegith, -o, =us (G). A hedge sparrow
aegl (G). Shining, splendid
aego (G). A goat
aegr, -o (L). Sick, diseased
aegypt, =us (L). Egypt
aell, =a, -o (G). A storm, whirlwind
aelur, -o, =us (G). A cat; tail-wagging
aem, -a, -ato, -o (G). Blood
aene (L). Bronze; bronze-colored

aeno (G). Terrible

aeol (G My). Aeolus, god of the winds

aeol, -i, -o (G). Quick-moving, shifting

aep, -i, -y (G). Tall, high

aequa, -bil, -li (L). Equal, level

aer, -ar, -e (L). Of copper, money

aer, -i, -o (G). The air, atmosphere

-aeresis (G). Take

aesal, =um (G). A kind of hawk

aesch, -o (G). Shame, ugliness

aesch, -r, -ro, -yn (G). Causing shame; ugly

aescul, =us (L). The Italian oak

aesio (G). Fortunate, lucky

aesta, =tis (L). The summer heat

aesthem, =a, -ato (G). Sensation, perception

aesthes, =is (G). A sensation, perception

aesthet (G). Sensitive, perceptive

aestival (L). Summer

aet, -o, =us (G). An eagle

aeth, -e (G). Unusual

aeth, -o (G). Burn; fiery

aethal, -o, =us (G). Smoke, soot

aethi (G). Burnt

aethri, =a, -o (G). Open sky, open air

aethusa (G). Burning; a vestibule

aeti, =a, -o (G). A cause

aeto; =aetus (G). An eagle

affini (L). Allied, related

affluen, =s, -t (L). Abundant, rich

ag (L). To, toward

aga (G). Very, very much

agall, -o (G). Adorn

agalli, -d, =s (G). An iris

=agalma (G). A pleasing gift; a statue

agan, -o (G). Mild, gentle

agap, =a (G). Brotherly love, charity

agaric, =um (G). A mushroom

agast, -o (G). Wonderful

agath, -o (G). Good, brave

agau, agav (G). Illustrious, noble

agel, =a (G). A herd

agen, -e, -i (G). Unborn, young

=ager (L). A field

agera (G). Not growing old

agglomerat (L). Collected, heaped up

agglutin, -at (L). Glued together

aggregat (L). Brought together

agili (L). Agile, nimble

agitat (L). Stirred up; quick

agla, -i, -o, =us (G). Splendor, beauty; splendid, brilliant

agm, =a, -ato, -et (G). A fragment; a fracture

agm, =en, -in (L). A stream

agn, -i, =us (L). A lamb

agn, -o (G). Pure, chaste

agnoi, =a (G). Ignorance

ago (L): Drive; (G): Lead; a chief, leader

agog, =ue (G). Lead, lead away

agon, -o (G). An assembly; a contest

=agora (G). A marketplace

agost, -o (G). The bent arm; an angle

agr, =a (G). Booty

agr, -i, -o (L). A field

agreiphn, =a (G). A harrow, rake

agrest, -i (L). In the country, growing wild

agreu, -o (G). Hunt, pursue

agreu, -s, -t (G). A hunter

agri (L). A field

agri, -o (G). Wild, fierce

agro (L). A field

agrost, =es (G). A hunter; a person living in the country

agrost, =is (G). A grass; a hunter
ai (see also ae, e, or oe)
aichm, =a, -o (G). A spear
aidoi, -o (G). Regard with rever-
    ence; the genitals
aiet, -o (G). An eagle
aig (G). A goat; a waterfowl
aigeir, -o, =us (G). The black
    poplar
aigial, -o, =us (G). The seashore,
    beach
aist, -o (G). Unseen
aithyi (G). A sea gull; a diver
=aix (G). A goat; a waterfowl
=ajaia; =ajaja (S Am). The rose-
    ate spoonbill
al (L). To, toward
al, =a, -i (L). A wing
alac, =er, -r (L). Quick, active
alao (G). Blind
alat (L). Winged
alaud, =a (L). A lark
alax, =a (N L). Alaska
alb, -i, -id (L). White
album, =en, -in (L). The white
    of an egg
alc, -ae (G). Strong; strength
alc, =es, -i (L). An elk
=alca (Ice). An auk
alced, -in, =o (L). A kingfisher
alcim, -o (G). Strong, brave
=alcyon (G). A kingfisher; a
    zoophyte
=alector (G). A cock
alectr, -o (G). Unmarried
aleiph (G). Unguent oil
aleo (G). Hot, warm
-ales (the ending of plant order
    names)
alet, -o (G). Grinding
aleth, -o (G). True, honest
aleur, -o, =um (G). Flour, meal

alex, -i (G). Ward off
aleyr, -o (G). Flour, meal
alg, =a, -o (L). Seaweed
alg, -e (L). Cold, coldness
alg, -e, =ia, -o (G). Pain
ali (L). Other, another; a wing
alia (G). An assembly
alien, -a (L). Foreign
aliment (L). Nourish; nourishment
-alis (L). Pertaining to
alism, =a (G). Plantain
alkali (Ar). Soda ash, alkali
all, -o (G). Other, another
allact (G). Change, vary
allagm, =a (G). An exchange
allant, -o (G). Sausage
allass, -o (G). Change, vary
allaxi (G). Crosswise
alle (Ice). The dovekie
allelo (G). One another; parallel
alli, =um (L). Garlic, onion
allo, -io (G). Other, different
alloth (G). Elsewhere
allotr, -io (G). Strange, foreign
alluv, -i (L). Wash against, over-
    flow; a pool
alm (L). Nourishing, refreshing
aln, -or, =us (L). The alder
=aloe (G). A kind of plant
alope, -c, =x (G). A fox
alp, -estr, -in (L N). Mountains
alphit, -o, =um (G). Barley meal
als (L). Cold
als, -o, =us (G). A grove
alsin, =a (G). Chickweed
alt, -i (L). High, tall
alter (L). Other
altern (L). One after another
althae (G). Heal, cure
alti (L). High, tall
altil (L). Nourished, fattened
altr (L). Other

altri, -c, =x (L). A nurse

aluc, -o (L). An owl

alucin, -a (L). Wander in mind,
  dream

alucit, =a (L). A gnat

alut, =a (L). Leather

alv, -i, =us (L). The belly, womb

alve, -ol, =us (L). A cavity, pit,
  socket

alysc (G). Shun, avoid

alyss, -o (G). Uneasy, restless

am, -a, -an, -at (L). Love; loving; loved

ama (G). Together

amabil, -i (L). Lovely

amaen (L). Charming, pleasant

amal, -o (G). Soft, tender

amalg (ML). A soft mass

aman, =s, -t (L). Loving

amanit (G). A kind of fungus

amar (L). Bitter

amar, =a (G). A trench

amaranth (G). Unfading

amarygm, =a, -ato (G). A sparkle,
  twinkle

amat (L). Loved; a loved one

amath, -i (G). Stupid, ignorant

amath, -o, =us (G). Sand; sandy

amaur, -o (G). Dark, obscure

amax, -i, -o (G). A wagon, carriage

ambi (L). Around, surrounding

ambig, -u (L). Doubt; doubtful

ambit (L). A going around, a circuit

ambl, -y (G). Blunt

amblo, -s, -t (G). Abortion

ambo (L). Both

ambros, =ia (G). Food of the
  gods; divine, immortal

ambul, -acr, -at (L). Walk

ambust (L). Burned up, consumed,
  scorched

amby, -co, =x (G). A cup

ameb, =a, -o (G). Change

amel (OF). Enamel

ament, =um (L). A thong, strap

=amia (G). A kind of fish

amic (L). Friendly, kind

amict (L). Wrapped up

amid, -o; amin, =e, -o (N: ammonia),
  ammonia

amm, -o, =us (G). Sand

=amma, -to (G). A knot

ammon (G My). African

amn, -o, =us (G). A lamb

amni, =s (L). A river

amnio, -n, -t (G). A lamb; a foetal
  membrane

amoeb, =a, -o (G). Change

amoen (L). Pleasant, charming

ampel, -o, =us (G). A grape vine

amph, -i, -o (G). Around, on both
  sides; double

amphiblestr, =um (G). A net; a garment

amphibol, -o (G). Uncertain; attacked
  on both sides

amphor, =a (L). A bottle, flask

ample, -ct, -x (L). Embrace

ampli (L). Increase; spacious

=ampulla (L). A flask

amput, -a (L). Cut away, cut off

ampy, -c, =x (G). A head band

amydr, -o (G). Dark, dim, faint

amygdal, =a, -o (G). An almond

amyl, -o, =um (G). Starch; a cake
  of fine meal

an (G). Without, not

ana (G). Up, throughout, again

ana (L). The anus

anact, -o (G). A king, chief

anagall, =is (G). A kind of plant

analog, =ia, =y (G). Proportion

anant, -o (G). Uphill, steep

anapno (G). Breathe again, rest

anapt, -o (G). Fasten, hang
anarrhich (G). Climb up
=anas (L). A duck
=anassa (G). A queen
anastomos (G). Coming together
anat (L). A duck
=anax (G). A king, chief
anc, =eps, -ipiti (L). Two-headed
anch, -o (G). Strangle
anchi (G). Near
anchyl, -o (G). Crooked, bent
ancill, =a (L). A maid
ancipiti (L). Two-headed
ancistr, =um (G). A fish hook
anco, -n (G). The elbow; a bend;
   a valley
ancor, =a (L). An anchor
ancyl, -o (G). Crooked, bent
ancyr, =a (G). An anchor
ander, -o, =um (G). A flower bed
andin (NL). Of the Andes
andr, -o (G). A man
andren, =a (NL). A bee
anem, -o (G). The wind
aneu (G). Without
aneurysm (G). A widening
ang, =ea, -i, -io, -o (G). A vessel,
   box, case
angel, -o, =us (G). A messenger;
   an angel
angin, =a (L). Something choked;
   quinzy
=angor (L). A strangling; anguish
angui, =s (L). A snake
anguill, =a (L). An eel
angul (L). An angle, corner
angust, -i (L). Narrow
anhel, -a, -it (L). Puff, pant;
   asthma
=anhinga (S Am). The darter or
   snake bird
ania (G). Trouble

anil, -i (L): Of an old woman;
   (G): Cruel
anim, -a (L). Life, breath
animal, -i (L). An animal
anir (G). A man
anis, -o (G). Unequal
ankyl, -o (G). Crooked, bent
ankyr, =a (G). An anchor
anlag (Ger). Lie on; a foundation
annal (L). Annual
annect (L). Bound together
annel, =us (L). A ring, a little
   ring
annu, -a, =s (L). A year
annuen (L). Nodding
annul (L). A ring
ano (G). Up
anomal, -o (G). Uneven, irregular
anomo (G). Without law, lawless
anophel, =es (G). Troublesome
anopl, -o (G). Unarmed
ans, =a (L). A handle
=anser (L). A goose
ante (L). Before
=antenna (L). A sailyard
anter, -o (NL). Former; before,
   in front of
anth, -e, -o, =us (G). A flower;
   brilliancy
anthem, =is (G). A flower
anthra, -c, =x (G). Coal, charcoal;
   a carbuncle
anthren, =a (G). A bee
anthrop, -o, =us (G). A man
=anthus (G): A flower; (L): A bunting, titlark
anti (G). Against, opposite
antia, -do, =s (G). A tonsil
=antiae (L). The forelock
antillar (NL). Of the Antilles
antiqu (L). Old
=antlia (L). A pump

antr, -o, =um (G). A cave, cavity
anu, -la (L). A ring
=anus (L). The anus; a ring
aort, =a (G). The great artery
ap, =ex, -ic (L). The tip, extremity
ap, -o (G). From, off, away
apate, -l (L). Trick; fallacious
=aper (L). A wild boar
aper, -i, -t (L). Open, uncovered
aper, -o (G). Not mutilated
=apex (L). The tip, extremity
aphan, =es (G). Unseen, invisible
aphe (G). Touch
aphel, -o (G). Smooth
aphod, -o, =us (G). Departure
aphr, -o, =us (G). Foam
aphrodisi (G My). Sexual desire
aphrodit (G My). Venus, goddess of
  love and beauty, born from sea foam
aphron, -o (G). Silly, foolish
=aphtha (G). An eruption, ulcer
aphthit, -o (G). Imperishable
aphthon, -o (G). Plentiful
aphy, -o (G). Suck
api, =s (L). A bee
apic (L). The apex, summit, tip
apic (G). A pear tree
=apium (L). Celery, parsley
apl, -o (G). Simple, single
aplat, -o (G). Terrible
aplys, =ia, -io (G). A sponge; filthi-
  ness
apo (G). From, off, away
apoceno (G). Drain
apocyn (G). Dogbane
apono (G). Painless, easy
apophys, =is (G). An offshoot, outgrowth
=apotheca (G). A storehouse
apparat (L). Prepared; a preparation
append, -ic (L). Hang to; an appendage

appet, -it (L). Desire
applanat (NL). Flattened
apri (L). A wild boar
apric (L). Exposed to the sun
apsi, =s (G). A juncture
apsinth, =us (G). Wormwood
apt (L). Fasten, adjust, fix
aqua, -ri, -tic (L). Water; of water
aquil, =a (L). An eagle
=aquilo, -ni (L). The north wind;
  northern
arab, -o, =us (G). A rattling
arabi (L). Arabia, Arabian
arach, =is (G). A leguminous plant
arachn, =a, -i, -o (G). A spider;
  a spider web
arad, -o, =us (G). A rumbling,
  rattling
arai, -o (G). Thin, weak
arane, =a, -i (L). A spider; a
  spider web
arat, -i, -or, -r (L). Plow
=arbor (L). A tree
arbut, =us (L). The strawberry
  tree
arc, -i, -o, =us (L). A bow; an arch;
  a box
arcan (L). Secret, hidden
arch, -aeo, -eo (G). Ancient
arch, -e, -eg, -i (G). First, beginning
arch, -i, -o, =us, =y (G). Chief,
  principal; a ruler; superior
arch, -o, =us (G). The rectum, anus
archae, -o (G). Ancient
archeg (G). First, beginning
archeo (G). Ancient
archi (G). First, beginning; chief;
  superior; ruler
archo (G). Chief, principal; a ruler;
  the rectum, anus

=archus (G). Chief, principal; a
  ruler; superior; the rectum,
  anus
-archy (G). Rule
 arci, arco (L). A bow, an arc; a box
 arct, -o, =us (G). A bear
 arctic (G My). Northern, arctic
=arctium (L). Burdock
=arcus (L). A bow; an arch; a box
 arcy, =us (G). A net
 ard, -i, =is (G). A point, arrowhead, sting
 ard, -e, -o (G). Water, irrigate
 arde, =a (L). A heron
 arden (L). Burning
 ardi, =s (G). A point, arrowhead,
  sting
 ardm, -o, =us (G). A watering
  place
 ardo (G). Water, irrigate
 ardu (L). Steep, difficult
 are, =a (L). A space, ground
 aren, =a, -i (L). Sand
 arent (L). Dry, thirsty
 areo (L): Dry, thirsty; (G): Warlike, martial
 areol, =a (L). A little open space
 aresc (L). Dry, thirsty
=arethusa (LN). A water fountain
 arg, -o (G). Shining, bright
 argem, -a, -at (G). An ulcer in
  the eye
 argemon (G). An herb
 argent, -at, -e (L). Silver; silvery
 argi, =a (G). Idleness, leisure
 argill, -o, =us (G). White clay
 argo (G). Shining, bright
 argyr, -o, =us (G). Silver
 ari (G). Much; very; warlike
 arid (L). Dry
 arie, =s, -t (L). A ram
 arill (NL). A wrapper

 arist, =a, -i, -o (L). An awn,
  bristle
 arist, -o (G). Best, noblest
 arithm, -o (G). A number
 arithm, -et, -o (G). Easily num-
  bered, few
-arium (L). A place where something is kept
 arma, -t (L). Arms; armed
 armill, =a (L). A bracelet
 arn, -o, =us (G). A lamb
 aro (G). Plow, cultivate
 aroli, =um (NL). A roll of cloth
=aroma, -t (G). Spice, seasoning
 arot, -o, -r, -ro (G). Plowing; a
  crop
 arpact, =es (G). A robber
 arqua, -t (L). A bow, rainbow;
  curved
 arrect (L). Steep, upright
 arrhen, -o (G). Male
 arrog (L). Assume, appropriate
 ars, =is (G). A raising, lifting
 arsen (G): Male; (L): Arsenic
 artam, -o, =us (G). A butcher
 artem, =ia (G). Something sus-
  pended; safety
=artemis (G My). Diana, goddess of
  the hunt
 arteri, =a, -o (G). The windpipe;
  an artery
 arthr, -o, =um (G). A joint; speech
 artic, -ul (L). A joint; speech
 artio (G). Even in number
 arto, =artus (G). A loaf of bread
 arunc, =us (L). The goat's-beard
 arundi, -n (L). A reed
 arv, -al, -ens, =um (L). A field
-ary (L). A place where something
  is kept
 aryten, =a (G). A ladle; a pitcher
 asbol, -o, =us (G). Soot

asc, -i, -o, =us (G). A bag, bladder

ascalaph, =us (G). An owl

ascari, =s (G). An intestinal worm

asce, -t (G). Practice; curiously wrought

ascend (L). Climb, mount up

asci (G). A bag, bladder

asci, =a (L). A hatchet

ascid, -i, =ium (G). A little bag

ascio (G). Without shade

asclepi, =us (G My). Aesculapius, god of medicine

asco (G). A bag, bladder

asell, =us (L). A little ass

asem, -i, -o (G). Obscure, indistinct

asil, =us (L). A gadfly, horse fly

asin, =us (L). An ass, simpleton

asine (G). Harmless, unharmed

=asio (L). An owl

aspala (G). A mole

aspalath, =us (G). A sweet-scented shrub

asparag, =us (G). Asparagus

asper (L). Rough

asperg (L). Scatter, sprinkle

aspers (L). Scattered, sprinkled

aspi, -d, =s (G): A shield; (L): An adder, viper

aspr (L). Rough

aspre, -d, -t (L). Roughness; a rough place

assul, =a (L). A splinter

astac, -o, =us (G). A lobster

=aster, -o (G). A star

=astes (G). A singer

asthen (G). Weak, feeble

=asthma, -t (G). Panting, gasping

astr, -o, =um (G). A star

astragal, -o =us (G). The ankle bone; dice

astrap, =a, -e (G). Lightning

astring (L). Bind together, fasten

astro (G). A star

=astur (L). A hawk

astut (L). Skilled, cunning

atalant, -o (G). Equal to

atav (L). An ancestor

=ater (L). Black

=ather, -o (G). The beard of an ear of corn

athet, -o (G). Useless, set aside

athl, -o, =um (G). A prize; a contest for a prize

athlet (G). A combatant, prize fighter

atla, -nt, -nto, =s (G My). A giant bearing up the pillars of heaven; the atlas bone

atloid, -o (G My). A giant bearing up the pillars of heaven; the atlas bone

atm, -i, -ido, -o, =us (G). Smoke, vapor

atop, -o (G). Out of place

atr, -i (L). Black

atrament, =um (L). Ink; inky

atrat (L). Clothed in black

atri, =um (L). A vestibule; black

atro, -c, =x (L). Hideous, terrible, cruel

attac, =us (G). A kind of locust

attagen, =is (L). A snipe; a grouse

attelab, =us (G). A wingless locust

attenuat (L). Thin, weak

au (G). Besides

auant (G). Wasted, atrophied

auchen, -o, =us (G). The neck, throat

auchm, -o (G). Drought

auct, -i, -or (L). Increase, produce; a producer, author; abundant

auctumn, -i, =us (L). Autumn

aucup, -al, -i (L). Bird-catching
aud, -ac, -en (L). Daring
audi, -en, -t (L). Hear
aug (G). Bright
augm, -en, -in (L). Increase,
  growth
augur (L). A soothsayer, prophet
aul, =a, -i (G). A courtyard, hall
aul, -o, =us (G). A pipe; a wind
  instrument
aula, -c, -co, =x (G). A furrow
=aulon (G). A pipe; a meadow
aur, =a, -o (L). Air
aur, -ar, -at, -e, -i (L). Gold,
  golden
aur, -i, -icul, =is, -it (L). An
  ear
auranti (NL). Orange colored
auricul, -o (L). The auricle of
  the ear or heart
aurit (L). Eared
auro (L). Air
auror, =a (L). Dawn
auscult, -a (L). Listen to
austr, -ali (L). Southern
aut, -o (G). Self
autumn, -ali (L). Autumn
aux, -e, -o (G). Grow, enlarge
auxili, -ari (L). Aid; aiding
avar, -i (L). Eager, greedy
=avena (L). Oats
avers (L). Turned away, with-
  drawn
avi, -a, =s (L). A bird
avid (L). Eager, greedy
avit (L). A grandfather; ances-
  tral
axi, =s (L). An axis, axle
=axilla (L). The armpit
axio (G). Worthy, good
axo, =n (G). An axle, axis
az, -ale, -o (G). Dry, parched

azot (F). Nitrogen
azyg, -o (G). Unpaired, unmarried

B

bacc, =a, -i (L). A berry; a pearl
bacch, -an, -e (G My). Wine; frenzy
bacill, =um (L). A little stick
bact, -er, -r (G). A rod, staff
bacteri, -o (G). Bacteria
bacul, =um (L). A rod, staff
badis, -i, -t (G). Walk, step
baen, -o (G). Walk, step
baeo (G). Little
bagn (It). A bath
baio (G). Little
balaen, =a, -i, -o (L). A whale
balan, -o, =us (G). An acorn; the
  glans of the penis
balane, -i, -u (G). A bath
balanti, =um (G). A bag, pouch
balb (L). Stammering
baleen (L). A whale
bali, -o (G). Spotted; nimble
balist, =a (L). A catapult
ball, -o (G). Throw, strike
ballism (G). Jumping about
ballot, =a (G). Hoarhound
balne, -ari, -o (L). A bath
balsam, -o, =um (G). A balsam
  tree; balsam
balteat (L). Girdled
bam (G). Go, walk
bap, -h, -t, -tis (G). Dye; dip;
  baptize
bar, -o, =us (G). Pressure; a
  burden
bar, -o, -y (G). Heavy
barb, =a (L). A beard
barbat (L). Bearded
barbar, -o (G). Foreign
bari, -do, =s (G). A boat
barnac (F). A goose

baro; =barus; bary (G). Pressure; a burden; heavy

bas, -a, -eo, -i, -o (L). A base, foundation; a step

basan, -i, -ism, -ist, -o (G). Test to prove genuine; torture

basi (L). Base, foundation; kiss

basidi, =um (L). A small pedestal

basil, -e, -ic (G). Royal

basi, baso (L). A base, foundation; a step

basm, -o, =us (G). A step, degree

bass (LL). Low, deep

bassan (L). Bass Rock

bassar, =a, =is (G). A fox

bat, =es (G). One that walks or haunts

bat, -o, =us (G). A bramble; passable

bath, -o, -y (G). Deep; high

bathm, -o, =us (G). A step, degree

bathr, -o, =um (G). A base, pedestal

bati, =s (G). The ray fish

bato; =batus (G). A bramble; passable

batrach, -o, =us (G). A frog

batt, -o (G). Stammer

bdell, =a, -o (G). A leech

=bdelygma, -to (G). Disgust, abomination

bdelyr, -o (G). Disgusting, abominable

bdesm, =a (G). A stench

bdol, -o, =us (G). A stench

bebel, -o (G). Profane

beber (L). A beaver

bebr, -o (G). Stupid

bech, -ic, -o (G). Cough

bel, -emn, -i, -o, =us (G). A dart, sting

bell (L). Beautiful

bell, -ac, -at, -i, -ic (L). War

belli, -d, =s (L). A daisy

bellerophon (G My). A hero

bellu, =a (L). A beast, monster

belon, =a (G). A dart, arrowhead, needle

belu, =a, -i (L). A beast, monster

=belus (G). A dart, sting

bembe, -c, =x (G). A top; a buzzing insect

bembi, -c, =x (G). A top; a buzzing insect

benac, =us (L N). A deep lake

bene (L). Well

benign (L). Good, friendly, kind

benth, -o, =us (G). The depths of the sea

berberi (NL). Barberry

bernicl, =a (ME). A goose

bero, -e (G). An ocean nymph

beryll, -o, =us (G). A sea-green jewel

besicl (F). Spectacles

besti, =a (L). A beast

bet, =a (L). The beet

=betonica (L). Wood betony

betul, =a (L). Birch

bex, -i (G). Cough

bi (L). Two, twice, double

biaio (G). Forcible, violent

biast, =es (G). One who uses force

bib, =e, -ul (L). Drink, drinking

=bibio, -n (LL). An insect

bibli, -o, =um (G). A book, paper

biblo (G). Paper

bibul (L). Drinking

bienn (L). Every two years

bili, =s (L). Bile; anger

bin (L). Two, two at a time

bio, =s, -t (G). Life

bittac, -o, =us (G). A parrot

bitum, =en, -in (L). Asphalt, pitch
blab, -o (G). Hurt, damage
blaber, -o (G). Harmful, noxious
blac, -o (G). Lazy, sluggish
blacic, -o (G). Stupid, indolent
blaes, -o (G). Crooked
blan, -o (G). Blind
bland, -i (L). Smooth-tongued,
  flattering
blap, -s, -t (G). Hurt, damage
blast, -em, -o, =us (G). A bud,
  sprout
blatt, =a (L). A cockroach
blatte (L). Purple
blechn, -o, =um (G). A kind of
  fern
blechr, -o (G). Weak, feeble
=blemma, -to (G). A glance, look
blenn, -o, =us (G): Slime; a kind
  of fish; (L): a simpleton
blep, -o, =sis (G). A look, glance
blephar, -id, =is, -o (G). An eyelash
blit, -o, =um (L). A tasteless
  vegetable
blite (L). Insipid; stupid
blosyr, -o (G). Grim, stern
blothr, -o (G). Tall, high-growing
bly, -s, -sm (G). Bubble up
bo, =a, -i (L). A water serpent
bo, -ar, -o, =s, -v (L). An ox,
  cow
boe, -o (G). Little; an ox
bol, =a, -o, =us (G). A throw,
  stroke
bol, -ac, =ax, -o, =us (G). A clod,
  lump
bolb, -o, =us (G). A bulb
bolet, =us (L). A kind of mushroom
bolit, -o, =um, =us (G). Cow dung
bolo (G). Throw; a clod, lump

=bolus (G): A throw, stroke, a clod;
  (L): a morsel
bom, -o, =us (G). A raised place,
  stand
bomb, =us (G). A buzzing
bomba, -c, =x (LL). Cotton
bombol (It). A bottle
bomby, -c, =x (G). The silkworm;
  silk
bombyli, =us (G). A buzzing insect;
  a bumble bee
bomo (G). A raised place, stand
bon (L). Good
bonas (L): Bison; (NL): a kind of
  bird
boo (G). An ox, cow
bor, =a, -i (G). Food, meat
borag (LL). A kind of plant
borass, -o, =us (G). Palm fruit
borbor, -o, =us (G). Mud, filth
bore, -al (G My). North, northern
bori (G). Food, meat
boro (G). Greedy, gluttonous
=bos (L). An ox, cow
bosc (G). Feed
bosc, =as (G). A kind of duck
bosi, =s (G). Food, fodder
bostrich, -o (G). Curl; a kind of
  insect
bostrych, -o (G). Curl; a kind of
  insect
botan, =a (G). Pasture, grass, fodder
botaur, =us (NL). A bittern
bothr, -i, -o, =us (G). A pit, trench
botr, -io, -y, -yo, =ys (G). A bunch
  of grapes
botul, =us (L). Sausage
bou (G). A cow, ox
boub, =on (G). The groin
boubal, -o, =us (G). The buffalo
bov, -i (L). A cow, ox
bracat (L). Wearing trousers

brachi, -o, =um (G). The arm
brachist, -o (G). Shortest
brachy (G). Short
bracte, =a (L). A thin metal plate
brad, -o, -y (G). Slow
branch, -i, =ium, -o =um (G). A
   gill; a fin; hoarse
=branta (Ice). A brant, goose
brassic, =a (L). Cabbage
brecc (It). Break
brechm, -o, =us (G). The top of the
   head
=bregma, -t (G). The top of the head
brem (G). Roar
brenth, -a, =us (G). A stately water
   bird; arrogance
breph, -o, =us (G). An unborn or
   newly born child
brev, -i (L). Short
brith, -o, -y (G). Heavy; a weight
briz, -o (G). Nod, sleep; a grain
broch, -o (G): A loop; (L): with
   projecting teeth
brom, =a, -ato (G). Food
brom, -o, =us (G). Oats; a stench
bromeli (NL N). The pineapple
bromi, -o (G). Noisy, buzzing
bromo (G). Oats; a stench
=bromus (G). Oats; a stench
bronch, -i, -o, =us (G). The windpipe
bront, =a, -o (G). Thunder
=brosis (G). Eating; food
brot, -o, =us (G). Blood, gore;
   mortal
brote, -o (G). Edible
bruch, =us (L). A wingless locust
brum, -al (L). Winter
brunne, -i (LL). Brown
brut (L). Heavy; stupid
bryc, -h, -ho, -o (G). Devour; roar

brygm, -o (G). Gnashing teeth
bryo (G). Swell; moss
bu (G). An ox
bubal, =us (G). A buffalo
=bubo (L). An owl
bubon (G). The groin
bubul (L). Of oxen or cattle
bucc, =a (L). The cheek
buccin (L). A trumpet; a shellfish
=bufo, -ni (L). A toad
bul, =es, -i (G). Will, determination
bulb, =us (L). A bulb
bulim (G): Hunger; (L): a mollusc
bull, =a (L). A bubble
bun, -o, =us (G). A hill, mound
buprest, =is (G). A beetle poisonous
   to cattle
burr (L). Red
burs, =a (L). A hide; a purse
bust, =um (L). A funeral pile
=buteo, -ni (L). A kind of hawk
butom, =us (G). A kind of water plant
butorid (NL). A bittern
butyr, =um (L). Butter
bux, =us (L). The box tree
byo (G). Stuff full
byrrh (L). Red, flame-colored
byrs, =a, -o (G). A skin, hide
byss, -o, =us (G). Fine thread; fine
   linen; the depths of the sea
byth, -o (G). The depths of the sea

C

caball, =us (L). A pack horse
cac, -a, -h, -o (G). Bad
cacali, =a (G). The colt's-foot
cacatu (Mal). The cockatoo
caco, =a (G). Excrement
cach (G). Bad
cachinn, -a (L). Laugh loudly
cachr, -i, -y, =ys (G). Parched
   barley

caco (G). Bad, decayed, diseased
cact, =us (G). A prickly plant
cad (L). Fall
cad, -o, =us (G). An urn, cask
cadaver, -i (L). A dead body
caduc, -i (L). Falling early
cae (see also ce and coe)
caec (L). Blind
caecili, =a (L). A kind of lizard
caela, -t (L). Engrave, emboss
caen, -o (G). New, fresh, recent
caerule (L). Blue
caesari (L). Hair, long hair
caesi (L). Bluish gray
caesp, =es, -it (L). Turf, sod
cal, -o (G). Beautiful
cala (L). Insert; summon
calam, -o, =us (L). A reed
calamistr, =um (L). A curling iron
calamit (L). Misfortune
calandr, =us,(G): A kind of lark;
  (NL): a weevil
calapp (Mal). A cocoanut
calath, -isc, -o, =us (G). A
  wicker basket
calc, -i (L). The heel; lime,
  limestone
calcan, -e (L). The heel
calcar, -e, -i (L). A spur; lime,
  limestone
calce (L). Chalk-white; a shoe
calceat (L). Wearing shoes
calci (L). The heel; lime, limestone
calcitr (L). Kicking
calcul, =us (L). A small stone
cald (L). Hot, warm
cale (L). Heat
calen (L). Warming, heating
calend (L). First day of the
  month; a month
cali, =a, -o (G). A nest; a hut

cali, -c, =x (L). A cup
calid (L). Warm, hot
calidri, =s (G). A shore bird
calig, =a (L). A boot
caligin (L). Dark, obscure
calio (G). A nest; a hut
=calix (L). A cup
call, -e, -i, -o (L). Hardened
call, -i, -o, =us (G). A beauty;
  beautiful
=callaea (G). A cock's comb
callid (L). Shrewd, clever
callio (G). More beautiful
callo (L). Hardened, thick-skinned;
  (G): beautiful
callun (G). Adorn, beautify
calo (G). Beautiful
calor, -i (L). Heat
calpi, -d, =s (G). An urn, pitcher
=caltha (L). A marigold
column (L). Deceive, trick
calv (L). Bald
=calx (L). The heel; lime, limestone
caly, -c, =x (G). The calyx
=calymma, -to (G). A veil
calyps, =o (G). A beautiful nymph
calypt, -o (G). Covered; a cover
calyptr, =a (G). A veil
=calyx (G). The calyx
cambi (L). Exchange
cambr, -i (L). Wales
camel, -o, =us (G). A camel
camer, -a, -o (L). An arch; a
  chamber
camp, =a, =e, -o (G). A bending; a
  caterpillar
camp, -o, -s, -to (G). Bending, flexible
camp, =us (L): A field; (G): a sea
  monster
campan (L). A bell
=campe (G). A caterpiller

campestr (L). Of fields

campo (G). A caterpillar; bending, flexible; a sea animal

camps, campto (G). Bending, flexible

=campus (L): A field; (G): a sea monster

can (L). Gray, ash-colored

can, -o, =um (G). A straight rod

canach (G). Noisy

canadens (NL). Of Canada

canal, =is (L). A canal, duct

canc, =er, -r, -ro (L). A crab; an ulcer; cancer

cancell, -i (L). Latticework

cand, -e, -id, -or (L). White, brilliant

candidat (L). Clothed in white

canescen (L). Becoming gray

cani, -n, =s (L). A dog

cann, =a, -ul (G). A reed

cannabi, =s (G). Hemp

cano (G). A straight rod

cano, -r (L). A song, melody

canon (L). A rule, model

cant (L). Song; sing

canteri, =us (L). A horse

canth (G). The corner of the eye

canthar, -i, -o, =us (G). A kind of beetle; a drinking cup

cantheli, =a (G). A pack saddle

=canum (G). A straight rod

canut (L). White, gray-haired

capac, -i (L). Amount contained

capell, =a (L). A goat

=caper (L). A goat; the smell under the armpits

caperat (L). Wrinkled

capet, -o, =us (G). A ditch, trench

capill, -a (L). Hair

capistr, =um (L). A halter, nosepiece, muzzle

capit, -i, -o (L). The head

capn, -o, =us (G). Smoke

cappari, =s (G). A kind of plant

capr, -e, -i (L). A goat; the smell under the armpits

capreol, =us (L). A support, prop, tendril

caprific, =us (L). The wild fig

caps, =a (G). A box, chest

caps (G). Eat quickly

capsul, =a (L). A little box

capt (G). Eat quickly

capul (L). A handle; a tomb

car (L). Dear, loved

car, =a (G). The head, top

car, =ex, -ic (L). A sedge

carab, =us (G). A kind of beetle

caran, -g, -x (Sp). A flatfish

carapac (F). A covering, shield

carb, -o, -on (L). Coal

carbas (L). Flax, linen

carcer, -a (L). A prison

carchar, -o (G). Jagged

carcin, -o, =us (G). A crab; an ulcer

carcinoma, -t (G). Cancer; an ulcer

card, -i, =ia, -io (G). The heart

card, -in, =o (L). A hinge, pivot

cardam, =um (G). A kind of cress

cardinal (L). Chief, principal; red

cardu (L). A thistle

caren, -o, =um (G). The head; a peak or crest

caret, -to (F). A kind of turtle

=carex (L). A sedge

cari, =es, -o (L). Rottenness

cari, -d, =s (L). A shrimp

caric (L). A sedge

carin, =a (L). A keel

cario (L). Rottenness

carn, -eo, -i (L). Flesh

carnif, =ex, -ic (L). An executioner

carot (G): Stupor; (L): a carrot

carp, -o, =us (G). The wrist; a
  fruit
carph, -o, =us (G). Straw, dry
  twigs
carpin, =us (L). The hornbeam
carsio (G). Crooked, oblique
cartilag, -in, =o (L). Gristle
caruncul (L). A bit of flesh
cary, -o, =um (G). A nut; the nucleus
casc (L). Old
case, -i, =us (L). Cheese
cassi, -di, =s (L). A helmet
cast (L). Pure
castane, =a (L). The chestnut
castig (L). Chastise
=castor (G). The beaver
castr (L). Deprive of generative
  power
casu (L). Fall; chance
casuar (Mal). A cassowary
cat, -a, -o (G). Down, downward
catabasi (G). Descent
=catagma, -to (G). A fracture; a
  piece of wool
catalysi, =s (G). A dissolving
catant (G). Downward, downhill
catari (LL). Of a cat
cataract (G). Falling down
caten, =a, -ari (L). A chain
=cathamma, -to (G). A knot
cathar, -o (G). Clean, pure
cathart, -i (G). Cleansing
cathedr, =a (G). A seat
cathet, -o (G). Hanging down,
  perpendicular
cathism (G). A seat
cathod (G). A going down, descent
catholic, -o (G). Universal
catill, -o (G). Roll up, fold up
catin, =us (L). A bowl, dish

cato (G). Down, downward, against
catopt, -o (G). Conspicuous, visible
catoptr, -o, =um (G). A mirror
catul, =us (L). A puppy
cau, -m, -s, -st, -t (G). Burn, burning
caud, =a (L). The tail
caud, =ex, -ic (L). The trunk of a
  tree
caude (L). Wooden
caul, -i, =is (L): -o, =us (G): A
  stem, stalk
caum (G). Burn, burning
caus -t (G). Burn, burning
caut (G). Burn, burning
cav, -a, -e, -i (L). Hollow, a cave
caval (F). A horse
cavern, =a (L). A cave, chamber
cavill, =a (L). Jest, jeer
ceanoth, =us (G). A kind of thistle
ceasm (G). A chip, splinter
ceb, -o, =us (G). A monkey
cebl, =a, -e (G). The head
cec (L). Blind
ceci, -do, =s (G). A gallnut; juice;
  ink
ceco (G). A sea bird
cecrop, -i (My). A king of Attica
=cedemon (G). A mourner; a guardian
cedr, -o =us (G). Cedar
celad, -o, =us (G). The noise of
  moving wind or water
celastr, =us (G). An evergreen tree
celat (L). Concealed
cele (G). A rupture, hernia; a
  tumor
celebr (L). Famous
celeo (G). A woodpecker; charm,
  bewitch
celer, -i (L). Swift
celest, -i (L). Heavenly

celet (L). Hidden

celi, -a (G). Hollow; the abdominal cavity

celi, -do, =s (G). A spot, stain, blemish

celib (L). Unmarried

cell, -a, -i (L). A granary, storehouse; a small room, cell

celo (G). A tumor; hollow; dry, parched

=celtis (L). A kind of lotus

celyph, -o, =us (G). A husk, rind, shell

cemet (G). A burial place

cen, -o (G). Empty; recent; common

cenchr, -o, =us (G). A kind of millet

ceno, -s, -t (G). Evacuation

cent, -e (G). Pierce, spear

cent, -en, -i (L). A hundred

centau, =r (G). A piercer, spearman

centes, =is (G). A puncture

centesim (L). The hundredth

centi (L). A hundred

centr, -i, -o, =um (G). The center; a point, spur

cep, =a, -ol (L). An onion

cephal, =a, -o (G). The head

cepph, =us (G). A petrel-like sea bird; a simpleton

=ceps (NL). The head

cer, =a, -e, -i (L). Wax

cera, -t, -to (G). Horn

ceram, -o, =us (G). Clay; an earthen pot

cerambyc (G). A kind of beetle

ceras, =us (L). A cherry

cerast (G). Horny; horned

cerat, -o (G). Horn

ceraun, -o, =us (G). A thunderbolt

cerc, -i, =is (G). A rod; a kind of poplar

cerc, -o, =us (G). The tail

cerchne (G). A kind of hawk

cercop, -i, =s (G). A long-tailed monkey

cerd, -al (G). Gain; cunning; a fox

cere (L): wax; (My): the goddess of agriculture

cereal (NL). Grain

cereb, -ell, -r, -ro (L). The brain

ceres (L My). The goddess of agriculture

ceri (L). Wax

cerin (L). Wax-colored, yellowish

cerith (NL). A shellfish

=cerma, -to (G). A slice; a small coin

cernu (L). Nodding, drooping

cerom, =a (G). Ointment

cert, -a (L). Struggle, contend; determined, certain

certh, -i (G). A tree creeper

cerule (L). Blue

ceruss, =a (L). White lead

cerv, =us (L). A deer

cervi, -c, =x (L). The neck

ceryl, =us (G). A kingfisher

cesi (L). Bluish gray

cespi (L). Turf, sod

cess, -a (L). Stop

cest, -o (G). A girdle; embroidered

cestr, =a (G). A pickaxe; a kind of fish

cet, -a, =us (G). A whale

cetr, =a (L). A shield

ceuth, =o (G). Concealed, hidden

chaem, -e (G). On the ground, low

chaen, -o (G). Yawn, gape; open

chaer, -i, -o (G). Delight, rejoice; a young pig

chaet, =a, -o (G). Long flowing hair, mane; a bristle

chain, -o (G). Yawn, gape; open

chalar, -o (G). Loose, slack
chalast, -o (G). Loose, relaxed
chalaz, =a, -o (G). A hailstorm; a
  tubercle
chalc, -eo (G). Coppery
chalc, -o (G). Copper
chalci, -d, =s (G). A fish; a lizard; a bird of prey
chalin, -o, =us (G). A strap,
  bridle
chalyb, -i, =s (L). Steel
cham, -ae, -e (G). On the ground,
  low
cham, -o, =us (G). A rein, bridle
chama (G). Gape
chan, -e, -o (G). Yawn, gape;
  open
chancr (F). Cancer
chao, =s (G). An abyss, empty
  space
char (G). Graceful
=chara (L). Cabbage
chara, -c, =x (G). A pointed
  stake; a sea fish
charact, =er (G). Something engraved
charadri, =us (G). A curlew
charadro (G). Full of gulleys
chari, =s, -t (G). Favor, grace
chari, -to (G). Graceful, favorable
chart, =a (L). A paper
=chasma, -to (G). A gaping
chauliod (G). With projecting teeth
cheil, -o, =us (G). A lip
cheim, -o (G). Winter
=cheir, -o (G). A hand
chel, -a, -i (G). A claw, hoof
chel, -on, =ona, -y, =ys (G). A
  tortoise, turtle
=chelidon (G). A swallow
chelydr, -o, =us (G). A water
  serpent

chem (G). Juice; pour; a yawning
chemo (G). Gaping; chemistry
=chen, -o (G). A goose; yawn, open
cheo (G). Pour
chern, =e (G). A day laborer
chers, -o (G). Dry; dry land
cheum, =a (G). That which is poured
chias, -m, -t (G). Cross, mark crosswise; diagonally arranged
chicor (F). Chicory
chil, -o, =us (G). A lip; fodder
chili, -o (G). A thousand
=chima, -to (G). Winter, frost
chimer, =a (G). A goat; a monster
=chion, -o (G). Snow
=chir, -o (G). A hand
chironom, =us (G). One who moves
  the hands
chit, =on (G). A tunic
chitra (H). Speckled; a deer
chlaen, =a (G). A cloak
chlamy, -d, =s (G). A cloak
chlan, =a (G). A cloak
chlani, -do, =s (G). A woolen garment
chlo, =a (G). A blade of grass
chloanth (G). Budding
chlor, -o (G). Green
=chlorion (G). A yellow bird
choan, =a, -o (G). A funnel
choem, -e (G). On the ground, low
choer, -o (G). A young pig
chol, =a, -e, -o (G). Bile; anger
chol, -o (G). Lame, maimed
chola, -d, =s (G). The intestines,
  bowels
choler, =a (G). The cholera
choli, -c, =x (G). The entrails
cholo (G). Bile; anger; lame, maimed
chondr, -o, =us (G). A grain, corn;
  cartilage
chondrill, =a (G). A lump

chor, -o (L): A chorus; (G):
  dance; a place
chord, =a (G). A string; the
  string of a musical instrument
=chordeiles (G). A stringed instrument
=chordeuma (G). A sausage
chore, -o (G). Dancing; go, with-
  draw
choret, =es (G). An inhabitant of
  the country
chori, -o, =on, =um (G). A skin,
  membrane
chori, -st (G). Asunder; separate
choro (L): A chorus; (G): dance;
  a place
choroid (G). Like a membrane
chort, -o, =us (G). A feeding
  place
=chrema, -to (G). Money, wealth
chres, -to (G). Useful
=chrisma, -to (G). An ointment
christ, -o (G). Anointed
=chroa (G). The skin
chrom, =a, -ato, -o (G). Color
chron, -i, -o, =us (G). Time; a
  long time
chrot, -o (G). The skin
chrys, -o, =us (G). Gold
=chthon, -o (G). The earth,
  ground
chy, -l, -lo, -m, -mo (G). Juice;
  flavor; chyle
chyt, -lo, -o (G). Fluid; shed
chytr, =a, -o (G). An earthen
  pot
cib, -ar (L). Food; edible
cibori, =um (G). A drinking cup
cicad, =a (L). A cicada, tree
  cricket
cicatr, -ic, =ix (L). A scar
cichl, =a (G). A thrush

cichori, =um (G). Chicory
cicindel, =a (L). A glowworm
cicinn, -o, =us (G). A curl of hair
ciconi, =a (L). A stork
cicut, =a (L). The poison hemlock
cidar, -i, =is (G). A turban
=cide (L). Kill
cili, -a, -o, =um (L). An eyelid,
  eyelash, small hair
cill, =a, -o (L). The tail
cim, =ex, -ic (L). A bug
cimbia (L). A girdle
cimeli, =um (G). A treasure
cimoli, =a (G). A white clay
cincinn (L). A curl, curl of hair
cincl, -o, =us (G). The wagtail
cinct (L). Girdled
cine, -ma, -mato, -s, -t (G). Move;
  motion, movement
ciner, -ar, -e, -i (L). Ashes
cingul, =um (L). A girdle, belt
cini, =s (L). Ashes
cinnabar (G). Red, vermilion
cinnyr, =is (G). A small bird
cinygm, =a, -ato (G). A floating
  body, phantom
=cion, -o (G). A pillar; the uvula
cipit (L). The head
circ, -a, -e (My). Circe, the en-
  chantress
circ, -i, -in, -ul (L). A ring, circle
circ, =us (G). A hawk that wheels or
  circles
circum (L). Around
ciris (G My). A bunting
cirr, =us (L). A curl of hair
cirrh, -o (G). Tawny, orange-
  colored
cirs, -o, =us (G). A dilated vein
cirsi, =um (G). A kind of thistle
cis (L). On this side
ciss, -o, =us (G). Ivy

cist, =a (G). A box, chest;
a shrub

cit, -i (L). Swift

cithar, =a (G). A lyre; a kind of
fish

citr, -in, -o (G). A lemon

=citta (G). A chattering bird; a jay

clad, -i, -o, =us (G). A branch,
sprout

cladar, -o (G). Fragile, brittle

clam, -a, -or (L). Cry out

clamb, -o (G). Mutilated, deficient

clandestin (L). Secretly

clangul, -a (NL). A clang, sound

clar, -a, -i (L). Clear

clas, -i, -m, -t (G). Break; broken;
a fragment

claster, -i, =ium (G). A knife

clathr (L). A lattice

claud, -i (L). Limp, lame; shut

claus, =us (L). An enclosed place

claustr (L). A lock, bar, door

clav, =a, -i (L). A club

clavicul, =a (L). A key

=clavus (L). A band on a tunic; a
swelling, wart

cleid, -o, =us (G). A key; the
clavicle

cleis, -is, -to (G). Close; closing;
closed

cleithr, =um (G). A bar, key, bolt

clem, =a, -t, =tis (G). A vine cut-
ting, twig, brushwood

clemen, =s, -t (L). Tranquil

=clemma, -to (G). A theft, trick

clemmy, =s (G). A turtle

cleo, -to (G). Glory; news

clep, -s, -t (G). Steal; a thief

clepsydr, =a (G). A water clock

cler, -i, -o, =us (G). A lot, portion; a kind of insect

clethr, =um (G). A key, bar, bolt

=clethra (G). The alder

clid, -o, =us (G). A key

clima, -c, =x (G). A ladder

=clima, -to (G). A region; the cli-
mate; a slope

clin, =a, -i, -o (G). A bed

clin, -o (G). Bend, slope

clio, -to (G). Glory; news

clipe, -o, =us (L). A shield

clis, -eo, -i (G). A bedroom; an in-
clination

clist, -o (G). Closed

clitell (L). A pack saddle

clithr, =um (G). A key, bar, bolt

clito, -r (G). Close

cliv, =us (L). A slope

cloac, =a (L). A sewer

clon (G). A branch, twig

clon, =us (G). A violent motion, a
tumult

clope (G). Robbery, fraud

clost, -er, -ri (G). Thread, yarn

clost, -o (G). Spun, coiled

clu, -d, -s (L). Close

clupe, =us (L). A shield; a river fish

clur, -in (L). An ape

=clydon, -o (G). A wave

clype, -o, =us (L). A shield

clys, -is, -m (G). Wash, drench

clyst, =er, -ero (G). A syringe

clyt, -o (G). Famous

cnec, -o, =us (G). Pale yellow; a
thistle

cnem, -i, -a, =is (G). The part of
the leg between the knee and the
ankle; legging, leg armor

cneo (G). Scrape, scratch

cnepha, -to (G). Dark, darkness

cnest, -i (G). A rasp, scraper

cneth, -o (G). Scratch

cnic, =us (G). A thistle-like plant

cnid, =a, -o (G). A nettle

cnip, -o, =s (G). An insect living under bark

cnism, =a, -ato (G). An itching

co, -l, -m, -n (L). With, together

coagul (L). Drive together; curdle

coarct (L). Pressed together

cobit, -i (G). A gudgeon-like fish

cocc, -i, -o, =us (G). A berry

coccin (L). Scarlet

coccy, -g, =x, -z (G). A cuckoo

cochl, =ea (L). A snail, snail shell; spiral; a spoon

cod, =a (L). The tail

cod, =ex, -ic (L). Writing, a manuscript

codia (G). The head

codon (G). A bell

coec (L). Blind

coel, -i, -o (G). Hollow

coeles, -t (L). The sky, heavens

=coelia (G). The abdominal cavity

coelo (G). Hollow

coemema (G). Sleep

coen, -o (G): Common; (L): dirt

coereb (Br). A kind of bird

coerule (L). Blue

coet, -o (G). Bed, sleep

coit, =us (L). A coming together

col (L): with, together; (G): the colon; a limb

col, -a, -i (L). Dwell

colapt, -o (G). Chisel, peck, cut

cole, -o (G). A sheath

colic, -o (G). Affecting the bowels

=colinus (Mex). The bobwhite

coli, -o, =us (G). A woodpecker

coll, -a (G). Glue

coll, -i (L). The neck; a hill

collari (L). Of the collar

collat (L). Brought together

collet (G). Glued together

colli, =s (L). A hill

collicul (L). A little hill

collig, -at (L). Bound together

collin (L). Found on a hill

collinit (L). Besmeared

collod (G). Glue-like

=collum (L). The neck

collyr, =a (L): Macaroni; (G): a small cake

colo (G). The colon; a limb; maimed, curtailed

colob, -o (G). Shortened, mutilated

colocynth, =a (G). A pumpkin

colon, -o (G). Shorten; the colon

colophon (G). The summit, end

color, -i (L). Color

coloss, -o (G). Gigantic

-colous (L). Inhabiting

colp, -o, =us (G). The bosom; the womb; the vagina

colub, =er, -r (L). A serpent, snake

columb, =a (L). A dove, pigeon

column, =a (L). A pillar

-colus (L). Inhabiting

colymb, -i, -o (G). A diver, a diving bird

com (L). With, together

=coma, -to (L): Hair; (G): a deep sleep

comi, -d (G). Care, attention

comm, -o, =us (G). Ornamentation; lamentation

comma (G). A short clause; a stamp, coin

commis (L). United

commun (L). Common; in common

=commus (G). Ornamentation; lamentation

comos (L). With long hair

comp, -o (G). Make a noise, clash; a noise

comps, -o (G). Neat, elegant

compt (L). An ornament
con (L). With, together
con, -i, -o, =us (G). A cone; a
   pine cone
conario (G). The pineal gland
conch, =a, -o (G). A shell
conchyli, -o, =um (G). A shellfish
condit (L). Hidden; polished
condyl, -o, =us (G). A knuckle,
   knob
cong, =er, -r (L). An eel
coni, -co, -o, =um (G). A cone; a
   pine cone; pine, hemlock
coni, -di, -o, =s (G). Dust
coniat, -o (G). Plastered, whitewashed
conjug (L). Joined together
connar, =us (G). An evergreen
   tree
conniv (L). Wink
cono (G). A cone; a pine cone
conop, =s (G). A gnat
conspers (L). Spotted, speckled
cont, -o, =us (G). A pole; short
contabesc (L). Waste away
contigu (L). Adjoining
contra (L). Against, opposite
contumac (L). Stubborn, haughty
conul (L). A little cone
=conus (G). A cone, a pine cone
convall, =is (L). A valley
convolv (L). Roll together; a bindweed
cop, -a, -e, -i (G). An oar, handle
cop, -o (G). Pain, suffering
copal (Mex). Blunt
coph, -o (G). Deaf; dumb; blunt
copi (G). An oar, handle
copid (G). A cleaver
copios (L). Abundant
copo (G). Pain, suffering

copr, -o, =us (G). Dung, excrement
copt, -o (G). Cut; strike
copul, =a (L). A link, bond
cora, -c, -co, =x (G). A crow, raven
corall, -i, =ium (G). Coral
corb, -i, =is (L). A basket
corchor, =us (G). Chickweed
cord, -i (L). The heart
cordul, -e, -i (G). A club; a swelling
cordyl, -e, -i (G). A club; a swelling
core (G). The pupil of the eye; a
   maiden
core, -i, -o (G). A bug; sweep
corem, =a (G). A broom; refuse
corethr, =um (G). A broom
cori, -a, =um (L). Leather, skin
cori, =s (G). A bug; a kind of fish
corm, -o, =us (G). A log, tree trunk
corn, -e (L). Horn; horny
corni, -c, =x (L). A crow
cornut (L). Horned
coro (G). The pupil of the eye
coroll, =a (L). A little crown or
   wreath
coron, =a (L): A crown; (G): a raven
corp, -or, -u (L). A body
corpusc (L). A little body
corrugat (L). Wrinkled
corrupt (L). Marred, spoiled
cort, =ex, -ic, -ico (L). The bark,
   shell
corthyl, =us (G). A crested bird
cortin, =a (L). A kettle; a curtain
corv, =us (L). A crow, raven
cory, -d, =s (G). A helmet
coryc, -o, =us (G). A sack
coryd, -o, =us (G). The crested lark
corydal, =is, •us (G). A lark; larkspur
coryl, =us (L). The hazel tree
corymb, =us (G). The top, summit
   a cluster of flowers
coryn, =a, -et (G). A club

coryph, =a (G). The head, top
=corys (G). A helmet
coryst, =es (G). A warrior
coryz, =a (G). A running at the nose
coscin, -i, =um (G). A sieve
cosm, -o (G). Order; the world,
  universe
cosmet (G). Well ordered, adorned
cost, =a (L). A rib
cost, =um (L). An aromatic plant
cothurn, =us (G). A high shoe, boot
cotin, =us (G). Oleaster, wild olive
cotone (NL). Quince
cott, =us (G). A kind of fish; a
  cock; a horse
coturni, -c, =x (L). A quail
cotyl, -ed, -o (G). A cup, socket,
  cavity
counter (L). Opposite, against
cox, =a, -o (L). The hip
=crabro, -n (L). A hornet
cracc, =a (L). A vetch
cracen, -t (L). Slender
-cracy (G). Rule; strength
cramb, -o (L): Cabbage; (G):
  parched
cran, -o, =us (G). A helmet
crang, -o, =on (G). A shrimp
crani, -a, -o, =um (G). The skull
cranter (G). A performer
crapul, =a (L). Intoxication
cras, -i (G). Mix, blend
crasped, -o (G). A border
crass (L). Thick
crastin (L). Tomorrow
crat, -ero, -i, -o, =us (G).
  Strength, power
crataeg, =us (G). A kind of thorn
crater, =a (L). A bowl
crati (L): Wickerwork; (G):
  strength, power
crato (G). Strength, power

cre, =as, -at, -o (G). Flesh, meat
crebr (L). Frequent, close
crecisc (L). A rail-like bird
crem, -a (L). Burn
crem, -a, -o (G). Hang
=cremaster (G). A suspender
cren, =a, -o (G). A spring
cren, -a, -ul (L). A notch
creo (G). Flesh, meat
crepi, -do, =s (G). A boot, sandal
crepit (L). Creak, rattle
crepuscul (L). Twilight
cresc (L). Grow, increase
cret, =a, (L): Chalk; separated;
  (G): Crete
=crex (G). A rail
crib, -ell, -r (L). A sieve
cric, -o, =us (G). A ring, circle
crin, -o, =um (G). A lily; separate
crini, =s (L). The hair
crinit (L). Bearded
crio (G). A ram
crisi, =s (G). A judgment, a choosing
crisp (L). Curled
crissa, -l (L). The under tail coverts
crist, =a (L). A crest
crith, =a (G). Barley
criti, -c (G). Chosen, select
croc, -e (G). A pebble; a thread
croc, -o (G). The crocus; saffron,
  orange-colored
crocid (G). The nap on cloth
crocodil, =us (G). A lizard, crocodile
crocut, =a (L). A hyena
cromy, -o, =um (G). An onion
cross, -o (G). A tassel, fringe
crotal, =um (G). A rattle, castanet
crotaph, =us (G). The temples
croto (G). Rattle; a tick
croton (G). A tick; the castor oil
  plant
cruci (L). A cross; torture

crudesc (L). Becoming raw
cruent (L). Bleeding, bloody
cruor (L). Blood
crur, -a (L). The leg, shank
=crus (L). The leg, shank
crusi, =s (G). A stroke on a
  stringed instrument
crust, =a (L). A crust, rind
=crux (L). A cross
cry, -mo, -o (G). Cold, frost
crybel, -o (G). Hidden
cryph (G). Hidden
cryps (G). Secret
crypt, -o (G). Hidden, concealed
cryst, -allo (G). Ice, crystal
cten, -idi, -iz, -o (G). Comb
cton, -o (G). Kill
cub (L): Lie down; (NL): Cuba;
  (G): a cube
cubit, =um (L). The elbow
cubo (G). A cube
cucuj (Br). A kind of beetle
cucul, -i, =us (L). A cuckoo
cucull, =us (L). A hood
cucum, -er, =is (L). A cucumber
cucurbit, =a (L). A gourd
-cul, =a, =um, =us (L). Little
cule, =us (L). A sack
=culex, culic (L). A gnat
culin, =a (L). A kitchen
culm, =us (L). A stalk
culm, =en, -in (L). A ridge, summit
culp, =a (L). Crime, fault, blame
cult (L). Cultivate, plow, till
cultr (L). A knife
-culu, =s, =m (L). Little
cum, -a, -ato (G). A wave
cumb (L). Lie down
cumul, -o (L). A heap, mass; form
  a heap
cun, =a (L). A cradle
cunabul, =a (L). A cradle

cune, -i, =us (L). A wedge
cunicul, =us (L). A rabbit; an underground passage
cunil, -a (L). A kind of plant
cunn, =us (L). The vulva
cup, =a (L). A tub
cupedi (L). Dainty
cupid (L). Desire; eager
cupr, -i, -o, =um (L). Copper
cupul, =a (L). A cup, cask
curcu (Ar). Orange-colored
=curculio, -n (L). A weevil
curr, -en (L). Run; running
curso, -r (L). Run; a runner
curt, -i (L). Short
curt, -o (G). Curved
curv, -i (L). Curved
=cuscuta (Ar). Dodder
cuspi, -d, =s (L). A point
custod (L). Guard
cut, -ane, -i, -ic (L). Skin
cyam, -o, =us (G). A bean
cyan, -e, -i, -o (G). Dark blue
cyath, =us (G). A cup
cybe (G). The head of a mushroom
cybern (G). Steer, guide
=cybister (G). A diver
cybo (G). A cube
cyca, -d (G). A kind of palm
cycl, -o, =us (G). A circle, wheel
cycn, -o (G). A swan
cydn, -o (G). Splendid, noble, famous
cydon, -i (G). The quince
cyem, -a, -ato, -i (G). An embryo
cyesi, -o, =s (G). Pregnancy
cygn, =us (G). A swan
cylichn, =a (G). A small cup
cylind, -ro (G). A roll, cylinder
cyll, -o (G). Lame, crippled
cym, =a, -o (G). A wave; an embryo
cymb, =a, -i, -o (G). A hollow vessel
cyn, -o (G). A dog

cynip, =s (G). A kind of insect
cyo (G). The foetus
=cyon (G). A dog
cypar, =is (G). The cypress
cyper, =us (G). A rush, sedge
cyph, -o (G). Bent
cyphell, =a (G). The hollow of
the ear
cypr, -ae, -i, -o (L). Venus; love
cyprid (G). Lovely
cyprin, -o, =us (G). A carp
cypsel (G). A hollow structure;
a swift; a beehive
cyri, -o (G). Master of; critical;
authentic
cyrt, -o (G). Curved, convex
cyst, =is, -o (G). The bladder;
a bag
cyt, =e, -o, =us (G). A hollow
place; a cell

D

dacn (G). Bite, sting
dacry, -m, -o (G). Tears, weeping
dactyl, -o, =us (G). A finger or
toe
daedal (L). Adorn; adorned
daict (G). Butcher
=dama (L). A deer
daped, =um (G). A level surface;
plains
daphn, =a, -i (G). The laurel or
bay tree
dapi, -do, =s (G). A carpet
dapsil (G). Plentiful
dapt, =es (G). Devour; an eater
dart, -o (G). Flayed, skinned
das, -i, -y (G). Hairy, shaggy
dasci, -o (G). Much shaded
dascyll (G). A kind of fish
dato (G). Divide, distribute
=daucus (G). The carrot

daul, -o (G). Shaggy
de (L). From, down, out
dealbat (L). Whitewashed
debil, -i (L). Disabled, weak
deca (G). Ten
decem (L). Ten
decen -t (L). Decent, proper
decid, -u (L). Falling off
decim (L). One-tenth; ten
decis (L). Cut off; settled
declivi (L). Sloping, bent down
decor (L). Elegant
dect, -o (G). Received; bite, sting
decuss, -i (L). The number "ten"
(X); a crossing
dedal (L). Adorn; adorned
=degma, -to (G). A bite, sting
dehisc (L). Split
dei (L). A god
deil, -e (G). Evening
dein, -o (G). Terrible
deipn, -o (G). A meal, dinner
del, -e, -o (G). Visible
dele, -t (L). Destroy
delect (L). Charming; a selection
delic, -at, -io (L). Pleasing, allur-
ing
deliquesc (L). Liquify
delir (L). Crazy
delo (G). Visible
delph, -i, -y (G). The womb, uterus
delpha, -c, =x (G). A little pig
delphi, -n, =s (G). A dolphin
delphini, =um (G). Larkspur
delphy, =s (G). The womb, uterus
delt (G). The letter "delta"; triangular
dem, -o, =us (G). People; fat
demas (G). A living body
demn (L). A bed
demono (L). An evil spirit
dendr, -o, =on, =um (G). A tree

dens (L). Thick; a tooth
dent, -i, -o (L). A tooth
dentat (L). Toothed
deo (L). A god
deon, -to (G). Necessity, duty
=depas, -tr (G). A cup, goblet, beaker
deph, -o (G). Knead
deplanat (L). Flattened
der, -o (G). The neck; the hide;
　old; flay
derm, =a, -ato, -o (G). Skin
dertr, =um (G). The membrane
　containing the bowels
desert (L). Solitary, lonely
designat (L). Marked
desis (G). A binding
desm, -a, -i, -io, -o (G). A band,
　bond, ligament
desud (L). Sweat greatly
detrit (L). Wear off
deuma, -to (G). Wet, soaked
deutero (G). The second
dex (G). An insect; a worm
dexi, -o (G). The right-hand side;
　clever
dext, -er, -r, -ro (L). The right-
　hand side; clever
di, -a (G). Across, through; sep-
　arate, apart
di, -s (G). Separate, apart; double,
　two
diabol, -o (G). Slanderous
diadem, =a (G). A crown, turban
diadoch, -o, =us (G). A successor
diadrom, -o (G). Wandering
=diaeresis (G). A division
diago (G). Transmission
dialy, -s, -t (G). Separate, break
　up, dissolve
diapedes (G). Leaping through or
　across
diaphor, -o (G). Different

=diastema, -to (G). A space, interval
diastol (G). Standing apart
diastroph, -o (G). Distorted
diathesi, =s (G). A condition, ar-
　rangement
=diazoma, -to (G). A girdle; the waist
dibam, -o (G). On two legs
dic (G). Right; a wood worm
dicell, =a (G). A two-pronged hoe
dich, -o (G). Two, in two
dichas, =is (G). A division
dichel, -o, =us (G). Cloven-hoofed;
　forceps
dicho (G). In two; split
dicr, -o (G). Forked
dicran, -o (G). Two-headed, two-
　pointed
dicrot, -o (G). Double-oared
dict (L). Say, pronounce, tell
dicty, -o, =um (G). A net
dicyrt, -o (G). Two-humped
didi (L). Distribute
didym, -o (G). Double, twin; the
　testes
=dieresis (G). A division
diet (G). A mode of living
difflu (L). Flow apart
digest (L). Dissolved; digest
digit, -al, -i (L). A finger or toe
dign (L). Worthy, fit
dilat (L). Expanded
dimidi (L). Half; to halve
dimin (L). Lessen
din, -o (G). Terrible; whirling
dio (G). Divine, noble
diphy (G). Of a double nature, two-
　fold
dipl, -o (G). Double, two
dipn, -o, =um (G). A meal, food
dips, -a, -i (G). Thirsty, dry
dipther, -a (G). Leather, skin,
　membrane

dir (G): The neck; (L): dreadful

dirig, -o (L). Direct

dis (G). Separate, apart; double, two

disc, -i, -o, =us (G). A round plate

discors (L). Discordant, disagreeing

disso (G). Double

dist, -a (L). Stand apart, be distant

ditto (G). Double

diure, -s, -t (G). Urinate

diurn (L). Daily, in the daytime

divaric, -a (L). Spread apart

diversi (L). Various; separated

divert (L). Turn aside

doc, -o, =us (G). A beam; a spar

doce (G). Seem; think

doch, -i (G). Receive; receptacle

dochm, -i, -o (G). Slanting, sideways

doci, -l (L). Teach; teachable

docim (G). Examine, test, prove

doco (G). A beam; a spar

doct (L). Learned, skilled

=doctor (L). A teacher

=docus (G). A beam; a spar

dodeca (G). Twelve

dodo (Pg). Foolish

=dogma, -t (G). An opinion, decree

dolabr, =a (L). An axe, mattock

doler, -o (G). Deceptive

doli, -o, =um (L). A jar

dolich, -o (G). Long

dolio (L): A jar; (G): crafty

dolo, -m, -p (G). Fraud, deceit, trick

=dolor (L). Sorrow

dom, -o, =us (G). A house

=doma, -to (G). A gift; a house

domestic (L). Around the house

dominic (L). Of a lord

dominic, -ens (L). Of St. Domingo

=dominus (L). A lord

dona (L). Give; a gift

dona, -c, =x (G). A reed

donesi (G). Trembling, shaking

dor, =a, -o (G). A hide, skin

dorat, =ium (G). A small spear

dorca, -do, =s (G). A gazelle

dori, -d, =s (G). A sacrificial knife

dorm, -it (L). Sleep

doro (G). A spear; a hide, skin; a gift

dors, -o, =um (L). The back

dory, -t (G). A spear; a beam, shaft

dosi (G). A gift

dox, =a (G). An opinion; glory

=draba (G). A mustard-like plant

drac, -aen, -o, -on (L). A serpent, dragon

drachm, =a (G). A weight

dram (G). Run

drama, -t (G). Perform; drama

drapet, =es (G). A fugitive

dras, -t (G). Act; an agent

drasteri (G). Active

drepan, -i, =um (G). A sickle

drimy (G). Piercing, stinging

drom, -a, -ae, -aeo, -i, -o, =us (G). Run; running; a race

dros, -o (G). Dew

droser, -o (G). Dewy

drup, =a (G). An over-ripe olive; a stone fruit

dry, -o, =s (G). A tree; oak

drym, -o, =us (G). Forest, woodland

drypt, -o (G). Tear, scratch

du, -o (L). Two, double

dubi (L). Doubtful

duc, -t (L). Lead

dul, -io, -o (G). A slave, servant

dulc, -i (L). Sweet

dulich, -o (L). Long
dum, =us (L). A bramble
duo (L). Two, double
duodec, =im (L). Twelve
duoden, -i (L). Twelve each
dupl, =ex, -ic, -ici (L). Double
dur, -a, -o (L). Hard
dya, -d, =s (G). Two
dyn, -am, -amo, -ast (G). Be
  able; power, energy
dyo (G). Enter, dive; two, in twos
dys (G). Bad, malicious, hard;
  enter, dive
dysis (G). Sinking; put on, clothe
dysporo (G). Hard to pass
dyt, =es (G). Dive, enter

E

e (see also ae, ai, o, or oe)
e (L). Out, without, from
-eae (the ending of plant tribe
  names)
ear, -in, -o (G). Spring, spring-
  time
eb, -en, -o (G). The ebony tree
ebri (L). Drunk
eburne (L). Ivory
ec (G). Out, out of, from
ecaton (G). A hundred
eccli (G). Bend down, turn aside
eccri, -s, -t (G). Separation;
  chosen
eccroust (G). Beaten out, driven
  away
eccye (G). Give birth to, bring forth
ecdem, -i, -io (G). Travel, go abroad
ecdys, =is (G). An escape, slipping
  out
ece, =sis, =tes (G). Dwell; a dweller
ecgon (G). Born, descended from
ech, -o (L). Reverberation of sound
echel (F). A ladder

echene, -i (G). Holding ships fast;
  a kind of fish
echi, -dn, =s (G). A viper, adder
echin, -o, =us (G). A hedgehog; a
  sea urchin
echm, -at (G). An obstacle, prop
echo (L). Reverberation of sound
echth, -ist, -o, -r (G). Hated; hatred
-ecious (G). A house
eclamp (G). Shine
eclip, -s (G). Deficient; leave out
eclog (G). Pick out, select
eco (G). A house, abode
ecphyad (G). An outgrowth, appendage
ecphyl (G). Alien, strange
ecphym, =a (G). An eruption of
  pimples
ecphys (G). Blow out
ecro (G). Escape; keep safe
ect, -o (G). Outside, out, outer
ecta, =sis (G). An extension, dilation
ectemn, -o (G). Cut out, weaken
ecthym, -o (G). Spirited, eager, frantic
ecto (G). Outside, out, outer
-ectomy (G). Cut out
ectop, -i, -o (G). Displaced, foreign
ectopist, =es (G). A foreigner,
  wanderer
-ectopy (G). Displacement
ectro, -m, -s (G). Abortion, mis-
  carriage
ecze, -m (G). Boil over
edaph, -o (G). The base, bottom; soil
ede, -o (G). The genitals
=edema, -t (G). A swelling, tumor
edest, =es (G). An eater
edibil (L). Edible
edr, =a, -i (G). A seat
ef (L). Out, from, away
efferen (L). Carrying away
effluen (L). Flowing away
effod (L). Digging; dig out

egeri, =a (L). A nymph
egi, =s (L). A shield, armor
ego (L). Myself, self
egregor (G). Watch
egresso (G). Watchful
=egretta (F). A kind of heron
eido (G). A form, image; like
eidol, -o (G). An idol, image
eir, -o (G). Wool
eis (G). In, into, toward
ejacul (L). Throw out
eka, -st, -sto (G). One, each
ekaton (G). A hundred
elacat, =a (G). A staff
elach, -ist, -y (G). Small
eleagn, =us (G). A marsh plant
elaeo, elaio (G). An olive; olive
  oil
elan, -o, =us (G). A kite; drive
elap, =s (L). A sea fish; a serpent
elaph, -o, =us (G). A stag, deer
elaphr, -o (G). Light in weight
elaps (L). A sea fish; a serpent;
  slipped away
elasm, -o, =us (G). A plate, metal
  plate
elasso (G). Make less
elat (L). High, lofty
elater (G). A driver
elatin, -o (G). Fir-like; a toadflax
elatr (L). Bark, cry out
elatri (G). Drive; driving
elc, -e (G). Draw, pull
elc, -o, =oma, -os (G). A wound,
  sore
elcysm (G). Dragging
elect (L). Choose
electr, -i, -o (G). Amber; elec-
  tricity
eleg (G): Mourning; (L): choice
elegan, -t (L). Elegant, fine
elench (G). Disgrace; test

eleo (G). A marsh; oil; distracted
eleph, =as, -ant (G). An elephant;
  ivory
elephant, -i, -o (G). An elephant
eleuther, -o (G). Free
elig (L). A choice; choose
eligm, -o (G). Winding, twisting
elis (L). Eradicated
-ell, =a, =um, =us (L). Small
ellip, -s, -t (G). Wanting, falling
  short; elliptical
ellop, -s (G). A sea fish; mute
elo, -d (G). A marsh
elop, -s (G). A sea fish; mute
elu, -d, -s (L). Get away from
elut (L). Washed out
elym, -o (G). A case, sheath; a
  kind of grass
elysi, =s (G). A step
elytr, -o, =um (G). A sheath, cover
em (L). In, into
embal, -lo, -m (G). Throw in, put in
emberiz, =a (NL). A bunting
embi, -a, -o (G). Lively, long-lived
embol, -im, -o (G). Inserted; a
  wedge
embrith, -o (G). Heavy, important
embryo (G). An embryo
emer, -a (G). A day
emer, -o (G). Domestic, tamed
emet, -i, -o (G). Vomit
emetic (G). Producing vomiting
-emia (G). Blood
emmel, =eia (G). A harmony, dance
emmen, -a, -o (G). Monthly; the
  menses; faithful
emolli (L). Soften
emphrax, -i, =is (G). An obstruction
emphys (G). Inflate
emphyt, -o (G). Implanted, innate
empi, -d, =s (G). A gnat
empir, -o (G). Experienced

empres, -i, -m (G). Burning; set
on fire

=empusa (G). A hobgoblin, ghost

empy, -ema (G). Form pus

emulsi (L). Milk out, exhaust

emy, -d, =s (G). A tortoise, turtle

en (G). In, into

enali, -o (G). Of the sea, marine

enall, -a, -agm (G). Differ from

enallax (G). Crosswise

enant, -i (G). Opposite

encarsi (G). Oblique

encephal, -o, =us (G). The brain

ench, -o, =us (G). A spear

enchely, =s (G). An eel

enchym, =a (G). An infusion

end, -o (G). Within, inner

endym, =a, -ato (G). A garment

endysi, =s (G). Entering; a putting
on

enem, -a (G). Send in

engraul, =is (G). A small fish

engy (G). Near; narrow

enhydr, =is (G). An otter; a water
snake

enhydr, -o (G). Living in water

enic, -o (G). Single

enne, -a (G). Nine

eno (G). Wine

enod (L). Without knots, smooth

-ens, =e, =is (L). Of, belonging to

ensi, =s (L). A sword

ent, -o (G). Within, interior

entas, =is (G). A stretching; a
spasm

entelech (G). Perfect

enter (L). Between, among

enter, -o, =um (G). The intestine,
gut

enthet, -ic, -o (G). Put in, implanted

ento (G). Within, interior

entom, =a, -o (G). An insect

enton, -i, -o (G). Tension; strained

entrop (G). Turn in, turn toward

enydr, =is (G). An otter; aquatic

enygr, -o (G). Watery, in water

eo, =s (G). Dawn; early

eol, -i, -o (G). Quick-moving;
the winds

ep, -h, -i (G). Upon, over, beside

epacr, -o (G). Pointed

epagog, -o (G). Enticing, bringing in

epan, -et, -i (G). Relaxing

epeir, -o, =us (G). The mainland, a
continent

ependy, -ma, -tes (G). A tunic

epenthes, =is (G). An insertion

eph (G). Upon, over, beside

epheb, -o (G). Youth

ephemer, -i, -o (G). For a day,
temporary

ephesti (G). Domestic

ephippi, =us (G). A saddle

ephydr, -o (G). Rainy, watery;
living on the water

ephyr, =a (G). A sea nymph; Corinth

epi (G). Upon, over, beside

epial, -o, =us (G). A nightmare; ague

epiblem, =a, -ato (G). A cover, cloak

epidemi, -o (G). An epidemic; among
the people

epidos, =is (G). An enlargement; increase

epier, -a (G). Pleasing

epilep, -s, -t (G). A laying hold of

epilept, -o (G). Epilepsy

epimach, -o (G). Assailable

epipast, -o (G). Sprinkled

epiped, -o (G). On the ground, level

epiphor, -a (G). An addition

epiphor, -o (G). Inclined, sloping

epiplo (G). A thin membrane, caul

epir, -o, =us (G). The mainland, a
continent

episio (G). Region of pubes; vulva
epistasi, =s (G). A stopping; attention
epistroph (G). Turn about; attention
epithalam, -i (G). Nuptial
epithe, -ca, -m, -s, -t (G). Added, laid on; covered
epithym, -i (G). Longing, desire
epitrop (G). Reference; a guardian
epomidi, -o (G). On the shoulder
=epops (G). The hoopoe
ept, -a (NL). Seven
epul, =um (L). A feast
epulot (G). Healing; a scar
epy (G). Tall
equ, -a, -i (L). Equal
equestr (L). A horseman
equi (L). Equal; a horse
equin (L). Pertaining to horses
equitan (L). Riding a horse
equu, =s (L). A horse
er (G). Spring; the earth
eran, -o (G). A contribution; a society
erann, -o (G). Pleasing
erasmi, -o (G). Lovely
erast, =es, -o (G). A lover; beloved
erat, -o (G). Lovely
ereb, -o, =us (G My). Darkness
erect (L). Upright
erem, -i, -o (G). A lonely place
erema (G). Gently, calmly
eresis (G). Take
eret, -mo (G). An oar; a rower
ereth, -ist (G). Irritate, rouse to anger
ereun (G). Probe, search
erg, =asia, -o (G). Work
ergat, =es, -o (G). A worker
ergot (F): Spur; (L): a fungus
eri (G). Early, spring; wool; very much; a hedgehog

eric, =a (G). A heath
erici, -n, =us (L). A hedgehog
=erigeron (G). A kind of plant
erin (G). A hedgehog; woolen
erio (G). Wool
eris, -m, -t (G). Quarrel
=erisma, -t (G). A prop, support
=eristalis (L). An unknown precious stone
ern, -o (G). A sprout; a child
erod, -i (G). A heron
eros (G): Love; (L): gnawed away
erot, -e, -em (G). Question, ask
erot, -o (G). Love
erotyl (G). A darling
erpe, =s, -t (G). Creep; a creeper
err, -an, -at (L). Wander; wandering
ers, -ae, -e (G). Dew; dewy, fresh; young
eruc, =a, -i (L). A caterpillar
erupt (L). Burst forth
erycin, =a (L). Venus, goddess of love and beauty
eryng, =us (G). A kind of thistle
eryo (G). Draw, drag
erysi (G). Red
erythr, -o (G). Red
es (G). Into, to
-es (G). (a suffix meaning an agent or doer)
-esc, -en, -ens (L). Becoming; slightly
eschar (G). A fireplace; a scab; a kind of fish
eschat, -o (G). Extreme, last
eschyn (G). Shame
escul, =us (L). Italian oak
esculen, -t (L). Edible
eso (G). Within, inward
esophag, -o, =us (G). The esophagus
esoter (G). Inner, interior
est, =es (NL). An eater
esth (G). Feel, perceive; clothe; eat
esthem, -ato (G). Perception

esthes (G). A garment
esthesi, -o (G). Sensation, perception
esthet (G). Sensible; a garment
esthi, -o (G). Eat
estival (L). Summer
estr (L). Belonging to, living in
estr, -o, =us (G). A gadfly; frenzy
estu, -a (L). Boil
estuar (L). The sea
-etes (G). Dwell; a dweller; one who
eth, -er (G). The upper air
eth, -o (G). Custom, habit; abode
etheo (G). Strain, sift; a bachelor
ether, -i (G). The upper air
ethic (G). Moral; national
ethiop (G). Ethiopian, African; dark
ethm, -o, =us (G). A sieve
ethn, -o (G). A nation
etho (G). Custom, habit; abode
etio (G). A cause
etiol (NL). Pale, whitish
etr, -a, -o (G). The belly, pelvis
-ett, =a, =um, =us (NL). Small
etym, -o (G). True; truth
eu (G). Good, well
euch (G). Pray
eudi, -o (G). Calm, clear
eulab (G). Wary, cautious
-eum (NL). A place where
eunuch (G). Guardian of the couch
euonym (G). Having a good name
eupatori, =um (G). Agrimony
euphorbi, =um (G). An African plant
=euphrasia (G). Delight
euphy (G). Shapely
eur, -o (G). East; the east wind; southeast; broad
eurin (G): Keen-scented; (L): the east wind

euro, -t (G). Mold
eury (G). Broad, wide
eustachi (N). Eustachio, an Italian anatomist
eutact (G). Orderly
eutel (G). Worthless
euthem (G). Orderly
euthy (G). Straight
euthym, -o (G). Generous
ev (G). Good, well
evacu, -a (L). Empty
evani, -d (L). Disappearing
evani, -o (G). Making trouble easily
evect (L). Carried out, led away
evectic (L). Good health
evira (L). Castrate
evolut (L). An unrolling
evuls (L). Pull away, pull out
ex (L). Out, off, from, beyond
exacerb (L). Violent, bitter
exagger (L). Heap up
=exanthema, -to (G). An eruption
exarat (L). Plowed up
excert (L). Projecting
excit, -o (L). Call forth, arouse
excresc (L). Growing up
excret (L). Separate, throw out
exeden (L). Eating out
exhib (L). Give, present
exhil, -ar (L). Cheer, gladden
exi (L): Go out; (G): habit
exigu (L). Short, small
exil, -i (L). Small, thin, slender
exo (G). Out, outside, without
exod, -o, =us (G). A going out
exorm, -i (G). Go forth
exoter, -o (G). Outside
exotic (G). Foreign
expir (L). Breathe out
expuls (L). Driven out
exsula (L). A stranger; an exile
extern, -o (L). Outside, outer
extim (L). Farthest away

extra (L). Outside, more, beyond, besides

extrins (L). From the outside

extrors (L). On the outside

exuber (L). Abundant

exud (L). Sweat

exust (L). Burned up, consumed

exuv, -i (L). That which is taken off

exygr, -o (G). Wet

F

fab, =a, -ell (L). A bean

fabul, =a (L). A fable

faci, -a, =es (L). The face; appearance

facil (L). Easy

=facula (L). A little torch

facult (L). Capability, skill

faec, -i (L). Dregs

fag, -a, =us (L). The beech

falc, -i (L). A sickle

=falco, -n (L). A falcon

fallac (L). Deceptive

fals, -i (L). False

=falx (L). A sickle

fam, -eli, -in (L). Hungry

famil (L). Friendly; a family

fantas (L). Fancy

farc (L). Stuff; stuffing

farin, =a (L). Flour, coarse meal

fasci, =a (L). A bundle; a band

fasciat (L). Banded

fascin (L). Charm, bewitch

fasciol, =a (L). A little bandage

fastigi, =um (L). Pointed; the point, top, summit; depth

fatu (L). Foolish, silly

fauc, =es, -i (L). The throat

faun (My). Faunus, god of agriculture and the shepherds

fav, -o, =us (L). A honeycomb

favill, =a (L). Embers

febr, -i (L). Fever; boil

fec, -i (L). Dregs

fecul (L). Foul; sediment

fecund (L). Fruitful

feli, -n, =s (L). A cat

felic (L). Favorable, lucky

fell (L). The gall bladder; bile

felo (L). A cat; a robber

fem, -or, -oro, =ur (L). The thigh

femin (L). Female, of a woman

fenestr, =a (L). A window

feng, -o (G). Light

fenisec, =a (L). A mower, harvester

fer (L). Bear, carry

fer, -a (L). Wild; a wild beast

ferment (L). Yeast, leaven

fero, -c, =x (L). Fierce, wild

-ferous (L). Bearing

ferr, -o (L). Iron

ferrugin (L). Rust-colored

ferrul (F). A ring, bracelet

fertil (L). Fruitful

ferul, =a (L). A walking stick; fennel

ferv, -en, -id, -or (L). Heat, burning

fess (L). Weary, feeble

festin (L). Quick

festuc, =a (L). A stem, stalk

fet, -i, =us (L). The young in the womb

feti, -d (L). Ill-smelling, putrid

-fex (NL). A maker

=fiber (L). A beaver

fibr, -in, -o (L). A fiber; a beaver

fibul, =a (L). A clasp, buckle

fic, =ation (L). Make, making

fic, -o, =us (L). The fig

fide, -l, -n (L). Faithful, trusting

fidi (L). A lute

fidic, -in (L). A lute player

figul, =a (L). A potter

figur, =a (L). A form, figure

fil, -i, -o, =um (L). A thread

fili, -a (L). A son or daughter
fili, -c, =x (L). A fern
fim, =us (L). Dung
fimbri, =a (L). A fringe, fibers
fin, -a, -i (L). An end, limit
firm (L). Firm, strong
fisc, =us (L). The state treasury; a woven basket
fiss, -i, -ur (L). A cleft
fistul, =a, -i (L). A pipe, tube
fivor (L). Bluish
flabell, =a (L). A fan
flabr (L). The breeze, winds
flacc, -id (L). Flabby
flagell, =um (L). A whip
flagr, -an (L). Burn, burning
flamm (L). Flame, burn
flamme (L). Flame-colored
flat (L). Blow, blown
flav (L). Yellow
flect (L). Bend
fleur (F). Flower
flex, -i (L). Bend; pliant
flexu (L). Winding
flig (L). Dash; strike down
flo (L). Blow
flocc (L). A lock of wool, flake
flor, =a, -i (L). A flower
floresc (L). Blooming
florid (L). Flowery
floscul, =us (L). A little flower
flu (L). Flow
fluctu (L). Wave, move to and fro
fluen, -t (L). Flowing
flum, =en, -in, -ini (L). A river
fluo (L). Flow
fluster (NL). Plait, weave
fluvi, =a, -atil (L). A river
flux (L). Flowing
foc, -i, =us (L). A point, focus; a fireplace
fodien, -t (L). Digging

foed (L). Filthy, ugly; an agreement
foenisec, =a (L). A mower, harvester
foeten (L). Fetid, evil smelling
=foetus (L). The young in the womb
foli, -a, =um (L). A leaf
folli (L). A bag, bellows
follicul (L). A little bag
foment, =um (L). A warm lotion
fon (G). Kill
fon, =s, -t, -tan (L). A fountain
foram, =en, -in (L). An opening
forcip, -i (L). Forceps
forf, =ex, -ic (L). Scissors
forficat (L). Forked
fori, -s (L). A door; out of doors
form, =a (L). Form, shape
formic, =a (L). An ant
formid (L). Fear
formos (L). Graceful, beautiful
forn, -ic, =ix (L). An arch; a brothel
fort, -i (L). Strong
fortuit (L). At random; fluctuating
foss, =a (L). A ditch, trench
fossil (L). Dug up
=fossor, -i (L). A digger
fossul (L). Burrow
fove, =a (L). A pit
fracid (L). Mellow, soft
fract (L). Break; broken
frag, =a (L). Break; a strawberry
fragm, =en, -in (L). A piece
fragr (L). Emit a scent
framb, -es, -oes (L). A raspberry
frang (L). Break
frat, =er, -r (L). A brother
fratercul, =us (L). A little brother
fraud, -a (L). Cheat
fraxin, =us (L). The ash tree
fregat, =a (It). A frigate

frem, -it (L). Roar, murmur
fren, -a, -at, =um (L). A bridle
frict (L). Rub
frig, -er, -id, -or (L). Cold
fringill, =a (L). A finch
fritill, =us (L). A dice box
frivol (L). Silly
frond, -e, -i (L). A leaf, foliage
=frons (L). The forehead, brow; a
   leaf, foliage
front, -o (L). The forehead, brow
fruct, -i, =us (L). A fruit
frugal (L). Economical, thrifty
frugi (L). Useful, fit
frument, =um (L). Corn, grain
frustr (L). In vain; deception
frustul, =um (L). A little piece
frut, =ex, -ic (L). A shrub
fuc, -i, =us (L). A seaweed; red
fug, -i (L). Flee, dispel
fuga, -ci, -x (L). Swift
-ful (E). Full of
fulcr, =um (L). A support, prop
fulg, -en, -i (L). Flash, gleam
fulg, -or, -ur (L). Lightning
fulic, =a (L). A coot
fulig, -in (L). Soot; sooty
fulm, =en, -in (L). Lightning; a
   thunderbolt
fulv (L). Reddish yellow, tawny
fum (L). Smoke
fun, -al, -i, =is (L). A rope
funct (L). Perform
fund (L). Pour
fund, -a, -i (L). A sling; the
   bottom
fune, -bri, -re (L). A funeral;
   death
fung, -i, =us (L). A mushroom,
   fungus
funi, -cul, =s (L). A rope, cord
fur, -en (L). Rage

furc, =a, -i (L). A fork
furfur (L). Bran, scurf, dandruff
furi, -os (L). Rage, madness
furn, -ari, =us (L). An oven
furor (L). Madness, fury
furtiv (L). Secret; stolen
furunc (L). A boil; a petty thief
fus, -i (L). A spindle; pour out
fusc (L). Dusky, brown
fust, -i, =is (L). A club, cudgel

G

gad, -o, =us (G). A kind of fish
gaea (G). The earth
gagat (G). Jet black
=gala, -ct, -cto (G). Milk
galag (Af). A lemur-like animal
galat, =ea, -hei (G). A sea nymph
galax, -i (G). Milky
galb (L). Yellow; a small worm
galban (L). Greenish yellow
galbul (L). An oriole; a cypress nut
gale, =a (L). A helmet
gale, =a, -i (G). A weasel, cat
galen, -a (G). Calm, rest; lead ore
galeo, -d (G). A shark
galer, (L): A cap; (G): cheerful
galgul, =us (L). A woodpecker
galid (G). A little weasel
=galium (G). The bedstraw
gall, =a (L). A gall nut
gall, -in, -o, =us (L). A chicken,
   cock
galvan, -i, -o (N: Galvani). Pertaining to the electric current
gam, -o, =us (G). Marriage
gammar, =us (L). A kind of lobster
gamet (G). A wife or husband
gamps, -o (G). Curved, bent
-gamy (G). Marriage, reproduction
gan, -eo, -o (G). Beauty, luster
gangli, =on (G). A knot on a string;
   swelling

gangren (G). A sore; gangrene
gargal, -o (G). Tickle; tickling
garrul (L). Chattering
gast, =er, -ero, -r, -ro (G). The
  stomach, belly
gaud, -e, -i (L). Joy; joyous
gaur, -o (G). Proud, majestic
gaus, -o (G). Crooked
gavi, =a (L). A sea bird, a loon
gavial, =is (NL). A crocodile
ge, -o (G). The earth
gecc, =o (NL). A chirping lizard
geiss, -o (G). A cornice, eaves
=geiton, -o (G). A neighbor
gelast (G). Laugh
gelat (L). Frozen, jelly-like
gelid (L). Cold
gelo (G): Laugh, laughter; (L):
  cold; freeze
gemin (L). Twin, double
gemm, =a, -ul (L). A bud
gen (G): Bear, produce; (L):
  a nation, race
=gena (L). The cheek, chin
gene, =a, -o (G). Birth, descent,
  race
gene, =sis (G). Origin, birth
genei (G). A beard
gener (L). Beget; a race; produce
genet (G). Birth, ancestor
genethli (G). A birthday
geni, -o (G). The chin, jaw
-genic (G). Producing
genicul (L). The elbow, knee,
  joint
=genista (L). A broom plant
genit, -i, -o (L). Beget
geno (G). Race, offspring; sex
-genous (G). Producing
=gens, gent (L). A clan, tribe
gentian (G). A gentian
genu (L). The knee

=genus (L). Birth, a race; a sort,
  class, kind
-geny (G). Production
geny, -o, =s (G). The jaw, chin
geo (G). The earth
gephyr, =a, -o (G). A bridge
ger, -o (L). Bear, carry
gera, -s, -t (G). Old age
gerb (Ar). A kangaroo mouse
=gerfalco, -n (LL). A sacred falcon
gero (L): Bear, carry; (G): an old
  man
geron, -t (G). An old man
-gerous (L). Bearing
gerr, -ho, -i, -o (G). A wicker
  shield
gery, -o (G). Shout; speech
gest (L). Carried
geus, -i, -t (G). Taste
gibb (L). Humped
giga, -n, -nto (G). Giant, very large
gigno (G). Know
gilv (L). Pale yellow
gingiv, -a (L). The gums
ginglym, -o, =us (G). A hinge
glab, =er, -r (L). Smooth
glaci, -a (L). Ice
gladi, -a, =us (L). A sword
gland, -i (L). An acorn; a gland
glani, =s (G). A kind of fish
=glans, (L). An acorn; a gland
glaphyr, -o (G). Hollow; neat,
  polished
glare, =a, -o (L). Gravel
glauc, -o (G). Gray, bluish gray; a
  kind of fish
glaucidi, =um (G). An owl
=glaux (G). Milk vetch; an owl
gle, -a, -o (G). Glue
gleb, =a (L). A clod
glecho, =n (G). Pennyroyal
glecom (G). Pennyroyal

glen, -o (G). A pit, socket; wonders
gleo (G). Glue
gli, -a, -o (G). Glue
gliri, =s (L). A dormouse
glischr, -o (G). Sticky; greedy
glob, -o, =us (L). A ball, globe
gloch, -i, =is (G). A point
gloe, -a, -o (G). Glue
gloi, -o (G). Glue
glom, -er, =us (L). A ball of yarn; a ball
glori, =a (L). Glory
gloss, =a, -o (G). The tongue
glott, -i, -o (G). The tongue
gluc, -o (G). Sweet
glum, =a (L). A husk, hull
glut, -i (L). To swallow; glue
glut, -e, -eo (G). The rump
glutin (L). Glue
glyc, -er, -o (G). Sweet
=glymma, -to (G). A carved figure
glyp, -h, -ho, -t, -to (G). Carve; carved, engraved
gnamp, -to (G). Bent, curved
gnath, -o, =us (L). The jaw
gnesi (G). Genuine
gnom, =a, -o (G). A mark; judgment
gnomon (G). Judge; rule; a carpenter's square
gnoph, -o (G). Darkness
gnorim, -o (G). Well known, familiar
gnos, =is, -t, -tic (G). Know; known; knowledge
gobi, =us (L). A kind of fish
gomph, -o, =us (G). A wedge-shaped bolt or nail
gomphi, -o (G). A tooth
gomphias (G). A toothache
gompho (G). A bolt, nail; bolt together
gon, -e, -idi, -o, =y (G). Seed, generation, offspring

gon, -i, =ia, -io (G). An angle
gon, -y (G). The knee
gonato (G). The knee
gone (G). Seed, generation, offspring
gongyl, -o (G). Round
goni, =a, -o (G). Seed; an angle, corner
gonidi (G). Seed; reproductive organ
gonim, -o (G). Productive
gono (G). Generation, offspring; seed; reproductive organ; the knee
-gony (G). Seed; reproduction
gony, -o (G). The knee
gordi (G My). A kind of knot
gorg (F). The throat
gorg, -o (G). Grim, fierce
gossypi, =um (L). Cotton
gour, =a (NL). A kind of pigeon
gracil, -i (L). Slender
gracul, =us (L). A jackdaw; a cormorant
grad, -a, -i (L). Step, walk; slope, grade
grall, -a, -ato, -in (L). Stilts
gram, =en, -in (L). Grass
gramm, -a, -at (G). A letter, writing
gran, -i, -o, =um (L). Grain
grand, -i (L). Large, great
grand, -in, =o (L). Hail, a hailstone
granul (L). A little grain
graph, -o, =y (G). Write, writing
graps, -i (G). A crab
grapt, -o (G). Inscribed, written
grat, -i (L). Pleasing; favor
grav, -e, -i (L). Heavy
gravid (L). Filled; pregnant
greg, -ar, -i (L). A flock, herd; collect
gremi, =um (L). The bosom

gress, -or (L). Walk, walking
=grex (L). A flock, herd
griph, -o (G). A woven basket; a
  riddle
grise (ML). Gray
griso (F). Gray-haired
grom, =a (L). A measuring rod
gross (L). Thick; an unripe fig
grossul, =a, -ar (LL). A goose-
  berry
gru, -i, =s (L). A crane
grum, =a (L). A little heap
gryll, =us (L). A cricket
grylle (Go). The black guillemot
gryp, -o (G). Curved, hooked,
  hook-nosed
guan, =o (Pv). Dung
guara (Br). An ibis
gubern, -a (L). A rudder; govern
gubernator (L). A pilot, gover-
  nor
gul, =a (L). The throat, gullet
gulos (L). Gluttonous
gumm, -i (L). Gum
gurg, -it (L). A whirlpool; en-
  gulf
gust, -a (L). Taste
gutt, =a (L). A drop
=guttur, -i (L). The throat
gyg, =es (G). A water bird
gymn, -o (G). Naked, bare
gyn, =a, -e, -eco, -o (G). A
  woman, female
gyp, =s (G). A vulture
gyps, -o (G). Chalk
gyr, -a, -o (L). Round; turning;
  a circle
gyrin, -o, =us (G). A tadpole

H

haben, =a (L). A thong, rein
habit (L). Live, dwell; fleshy
=habitus (L). The external aspect
habr, -o (G). Dainty, delicate,
  pretty

hadr, -o (G). Thick, stout
hadryn (G). Ripen
haed, =us (L). A young goat
haem, =a, -ato, -o (G). Blood
haer, -esi (G). Take
hagi, -o (G). Sacred
hal, -a, -e, -it (L). Breathe,
  breathing
=halcyon (G). A kingfisher
halec, -o (L). A herring
hali, -o (G). The sea
halin, -o (G). Made of salt
halia (G). An assembly
haliaet, -e, =us (G). A sea eagle,
  osprey
halio (G). The sea
halit (L). Breathing
hallo (G). Other; leaping
hallu, -c, =x (NL). The great toe
hallucinat (L). To wander in mind
halma, -to (G). Leap, spring
halo (G): The sea; salt; (L): breathe
halter (G). A leaping weight
haltic (G). Good at leaping, nimble
halys, -i, =is (G). A chain, bond
ham, -at, -i (L). A hook; hooked
hama (G). All together, at the same
  time
hamamel, =is (G). A tree with pear-
  like fruit
hamarti, =a (G). A fault, sin, error
hamat (L). Hooked
hami (L). A hook
hamm, -o (G). Sand
=hamma, -to (G). A knot, noose
hamul (L). A little hook
hapal, -o (G). Gentle, soft
haph, -o (G). Touch, grasp
hapl, -o (G). Simple, single
haplom, =a (G). A coverlet
hapt, -o (G). Fastened
=harelda (Ice). A sea duck
harmo (G). A joint; harmony
harmon, -i (G). Music

harp, =e, -i (G). A sickle; a bird of prey
harpa (LL). A harp
harpac, -t (G). Rob, seize
harpag, -i (G). A hook
=harpe, harpi (G). A sickle; a bird of prey
=hasta, -t (L). A spear; spear-shaped
hathr, -o (G). Heaped, assembled
haust, -or, -r (L). Draw up, suck
hebdom, -at (G). The seventh
hebe, -t (L): Blunt; (G): youth, puberty
heca (G). Far off
hecat, -o, =on (G). A hundred
hecist, -o (G). Least
hect, -o (G). A hundred; the sixth
hed, -i, -o (G). A seat, dwelling place
hede (G). Sweet
hedeom, =a (G). Sweet-smelling
heder, =a (L). Ivy
hedi, hedo (G). A seat, dwelling place
hedon (G). Pleasure, delight
hedr, =a, -io (G). A seat; the anus
hedy, -l (G). Sweet
hel, -a, -eo, -o (G). A bog, marsh
helco (G). A sore; suck
heleni, =um (G). A kind of plant
heleo (G). A marsh, bog; pity
heli, -a, -o (G). The sun
helic, -o (G). A spiral, coil
helict (G). Wreathed, twisted
=heligma, -to (G). A winding, wrapper; a curl of hair
helio (G). The sun
heliot, -h, =us (G). The moon
=helix (G). A spiral, coil
hell, -a, -ado, -en (G). Greece
hellu, -o (L). A glutton

helmin, =s, -th (G). A worm
helo (G). A nail, wart; a marsh
helo, -d (G). A marsh
helv (L). Tawny, yellowish
hem, -a, -ato, =ia, -o (G). Blood
hemer, =a, -o (G). A day; tamed
hemi (G). One-half
hen, -o (G). A year; a year old
hendeca (G). Eleven
henic, -o (G). Single
henicm, -o (G). Humid
heno (G). A year; a year old
hepa, =r, -t, -to (G). The liver
hepial, -o, =us (G). A nightmare
hept, -a (G). Seven
heracle (G My). Hercules, a mythological hero
herb, =a, -i, -o (L). Grass
herc, -o, =us (G). A wall, fence
hered (L). An heir; inherit; hereditary
herm, -a, -et (ML). Male; secret
=herma, -to (G). A prop, support
hermaphrodit (G My). With both male and female organs
hermin, -o, =s (G). A prop, support
hermos (Sp). Beautiful
herni, =a (L). A rupture
hero (G). A hero
herodi (G). A heron
herpes, -t (G). Creep, creeping; herpes
herpet, -o (G). A reptile
hesit, -a (L). Stick fast
hesper, -i (G). Evening; western
hestho (G). Clothing, dress
hesych, -o (G). Still, quiet
hesychast (G). A hermit
heta, -er, -ir (G). A companion
heter, -o (G). Other, different
heur (G). Invent, discover
hex, -a (G). Six
hex, -i, -io, =is, -y (G). Habit

hiat, =us (L). An opening, gap
hibern, =us (L). Winter
hibisc, =us (G). The marsh mallow
hicori, =a (NL). Hickory
hidro (G). Sweat
hidry, -s, -t (G). Seated, fixed
hiem, -al (L). Winter
hier, -o (G). Sacred
hiera, -c, =x (G). A hawk
hil, =um (L). A trifle, a little
  thing
hilar (L). Gay, cheerful
himant, -o (G). A strap
himati, =um (G). A cloak
himer, -o (G). Lovely; yearning
hipp, -e, -o, =us (G). A horse
hippari, =um (G). A pony
=hippocampus (G). A fabulous sea
  monster
hirc, -in, =us (L). A goat
hirne, =a (L). A jug
hirp, =ex, -ic (L). A harrow
hirsut (L). Hairy, rough
hirt (L). Hairy, rough
hirud, -in, =o (L). A leech
hirund, -in, =o (L). A swallow
hisc (L). Open
hispan, -i (L). Spain; Spanish
hispid (L). Hairy, bristly
hist, -o (G). A web; tissue
=hister (L). An actor
histero (G). Behind
histi, -o, =um (G). A little web;
  a sheet
histo (G). A web; tissue
histor, -i (L). History
=histrio, -ni (L). An actor
hod, -o, =us (G). A way, path
hol, -o (G). Whole
holc, -o (G). A furrow, trail;
  attractive; a grain

holothur, -i, =um (G). A kind of
  zoophyte
hom, -eo, -o, -oeo, -oio (G). Like,
  same, alike
hom, -in, =o (L). Man
homalo (G). Even, level
homar (OF). A lobster
homeo (G). Like, resembling, alike
homin, -i (L). Man
=homo (L). Man
homo, -eo, -io (G). Like, resembling,
  alike
hopl, -i, -o, =um (G). Armor, weapons
hople (G). A hoof
hoplist (G). Armed
hoplit (G). Heavily armed
hoplo, hoplum (G). Armor, weapons
horde, =um (L). Barley
horiz (G). Horizon; bound
hormi (G). Start, onset
hormo (G). A chain
hormon (G). Excite
horo (G). A limit, boundary; season,
  hour, time
horre, -n, -s (L). Dreadful; bristle,
  stand on end, tremble
horre, =um (L). A storehouse
horri (L). Terror; to bristle
horrib (L). Terrible, fearful
horrid (L). Rough, prickly
hort (L). Urge
hort, -i, =us (L). A garden
hosp, -it (L). A guest
hosti (L). An enemy
hum, -at, -i (L). Earth, ground;
  bury
human (L). Of a man
humer, -o, =us (L). The shoulder
humesc (L). Grow moist
humi (L). Ground, earth
humid, -i (L). Moist; moisture
humil, -i (L). Low

humor (L). Moist; a fluid
humul, =us (L). The hop plant
hy (G). U-shaped, Y-shaped
hy, -aen, -en, -o (G). A pig, hog
hyal, -i, -in, -o (G). Glass;
  transparent
hybo (G). A hump; hump-backed
hybrid, =a (L). A mongrel, hybrid
hydat, -in (G). Water; watery
hydn, =um (G). A fungus
hydr, =a, -i, -o (G). Water
=hydra (G). Water; a sea serpent
hydrargyr, -o, =us (G). Mercury
=hydrus (G). A water snake
hyem, -al (L). Winter
hyen, =a (G). A pig, hog; a hyena
hyet, -o (G). Rain
hyg, -ei, -ie, -io (G). Health
hygr, -o (G). Moist, wet
hyl, =a, -o (G). Matter, stuff;
  wood, woods
hylact (G). Bark, yelp
hylurg, -o, =us (G). A carpenter
=hymen, -o (G). A membrane
hymn, -o (G). A hymn, song
hyo (G). A pig, hog; U-shaped,
  Y-shaped; hyoid
hyp, -o (G). Under, beneath
hypen, =a (G). A moustache
hypenanti (G). Opposite
hyper (G). Over, above; excessive
hyper, -o (G). The palate; a
  pestle
hyperbore (G). Of the extreme north
hyperic, =um (G). St. John's-wort
hyph, -a, -o (G). A web; weaving
hyphaem, -o (G). Bloodshot
hyphaen (G). Weave
hyphant, -r (G). Woven; a weaver
hypho (G). A web; weaving
hyphydr (G). Found in water, under water

hypn, -o (G). Sleep; a moss
hypo (G). Under, beneath
hyponom (G). Underground; mine
hyps, -i, -o (G). High, on high
hyra, -c, =x (G). A shrewmouse
hyssop (G). An aromatic herb
hyster, -o (G). Latter, lower; the
  uterus, womb
hystri, -c, =x (G). A porcupine

I

iachr, -o (G). Softened
=iama, -to (G). A medicine, remedy
ianth, -in (G). Violet-colored
iapy, -g, =x (G). The west-northwest
  wind
-iasis (G). Treatment, cure; formation of, presence of
iati (G). Healing
iatr, -a, -ic, -o, =us (G). A physician
iatreus, =is (G). A treatment
iber, -i, =ia, -o (G). Spain
iberi, -d, =s (G). A kind of cress
=ibex (L). A kind of goat
ibi, -d, =s (L). An ibis
ibidem (L). The same
icel, -o (G). Resembling
ichn, -i, -o (G). Track, trace
ichneum, -on (G). A tracker; a
  kind of wasp
ichor (G). Juice, lymph, serum
ichthy, -o, =s (G). A fish
-icle (L). Little
icma, -le (G). Fluid, moist
ico (G). Likely
=icon, -i, -o (L). An image
icos, -i (G). Twenty
icter, -i, -o, =us (G). Jaundice; an
  oriole
icti, -d, =s (G). A marten, weasel
ictin, =us (G). A kite
-icul, =a, =um =us (L). Small

-id (L). A condition of

-idae (the ending of animal family names)

ident, -i (L). Repeatedly

ideo (G). Form, appearance

-idi, =a, =um, =us (G). Small

idio (G). One's own, peculiar

ido (G). Sweat

idol, -o (G). An image, phantom

idr, -o (G). Sweat; gum, resin

idri (G). Skilled

ign, -e, -i (L). Fire

il (L). Not, without; in, into

ile, -o (L): The intestine; (G): twist, roll; twisted

=ilema, -t (G). A covering, wrapper; a coil; a vault

=ilex (L). The holm oak

ilia, -co (L). The flank, loin

ilic (L). The holm oak

ilio (L): Intestine; (G): twist, roll

-ill, =a, =um, =us (L). Small

illaen (G). Squint

illat (L). Inferred

illici (L). Allure, entice

illigat (L). Fastened

illo (G). Squinting

illot (L). Dirty, unwashed

-illum (L). Small

illumina (L). Light up

-illus (L). Small

illusi (L). Mocking

illustr, -a, -i (L). Bright, made clear; distinguished

ily, -o, =s (G). Mud

im (L). Not; in, into

imag, -in, =o (L). An image, likeness

imb, =er, -r (L). Rain

imbecill (L). Weak, feeble

imbric, -a, -i (L). A roof tile, shingle

imbut (L). Stained

imita (L). Imitate, copy

immun, -i, -o (L). Safe, free; immunity

impar, -i (L). Unequal

impet, =us (L). An attack

implex (L). Twisted

in (L). In, into; not, without; on

-inae (the ending of animal subfamily and plant subtribe names)

inaequal, -i (L). Unequal

inan, -i (L). Empty

inca (Pv). Of Peru

incan (L). Hoary, gray

incert (L). Uncertain

incest (L). Impure, sinful, polluted

incho (L). Begin

incil, -i (L). A ditch; cut in

incis (L). Cut in, cut into

incol, =a (L). An inhabitant

incrass (L). Thickened

incu, -d, =s (L). An anvil

incub (L). Lie upon

=index (L). That which points out

indi (L). In; indigo

indic (L). That which points out; Indian; indigo

indig (Sp). Deep violet blue

indigen (L). Native; need, want

indo (L). Of India; indigo

indu, -t (L). Clothe; clothed

industri (L). Diligent

-ineae (the ending of plant suborder names)

inebri, -at (L). Drunk

inept (L). Absurd, foolish

infan, =s, -ti (L). A child, infant; speechless

infarct (L). Filled in, stuffed

infelic (L). Unhappy, unfortunate

infer, -o (L). Low, underneath

infloresc (L). Begin to bloom

infra (L). Below, beneath

infract (L). Broken, bent
inful, =a (L). A band, bandage
infumat (L). Smoked, smoky
infundibul, =um (L). A funnel
infus (L). Pour in
infuscat (L). Darkened
ingen, =s, -ti (L). Large, remarkable
ingluv, -i (L). The crop, stomach
inguin, -o (L). The groin
-ini (the ending of animal tribe names)
ini, =a (S Am). A kind of porpoise
ini, -a, -o, =um (G). The occiput, nape
innoc, -en, -u (L). Harmless
ino (G). A fiber; muscle; the occiput
inocul, -a (L). Implant
inquilin, =us (L). A tenant
insect (L). Cut into
insecti (L). An insect
insidi (L). Ambush; sitting upon
insipid (L). Tasteless
instar (L). A form, likeness
instig, -a (L). Stimulate
insul, =a (L). An island
integ, -r (L). Whole, complete; repair
inter (L). Between, among
intercal, -a (L). Insert
intestin, =um (L). The intestine
inti (L). Within, into
intim, -a (L). Innermost
intort (L). Twisted, distorted
intr, -a (L). Within, inside
intric (L). Perplexing
intrins (L). Contained within
intro (L). Within; in, into
inul, =a (L). A kind of plant
inuncan, -t (L). Hooked
inunct (L). Smeared
inundat (L). Overflowed, flooded

inust (L). Burned
involucr, =um (L). A wrapper
involut (L). Wrapped up; intricate
iod, -i, -o (G). Violet
-iol, =a, =um, =us (L). Little
-ion (G). A going or entering; small
ion, -o (G). Violet
ionth, -o (G). The down on the face
ios (G). Poison; an arrow
ip, -o, =s (G). A worm
iphi (G). Mightily, strongly
iphthim, -o (G). Spirited, stalwart
ipn, -o (G). An oven, furnace
ipo, =ips (G). A worm
ips, -o (G). Ivy
ipsi (NL). Same
ir (L). Not, without; in, into
ira, -sc (L). Anger; angry
iren (G). Peace
iri, -d, -do, =s, -t (G). A rainbow; the iris of the eye; a kind of lily
irrig, -a, -u (L). Lead water to
irris, -i, -or (L). Mock, deride; a mocker
irrit (L). Excite; useless
irror, -a (L). Sprinkle with dew
is, -o (G). Equal
isabell (N: Queen Isabella). Buff brown
isati, =s (G). A milky-juiced herb
isch, -o (G). Hold, suppress
ischi, -a, -o, =um (G). The hip, hip joint
ischn, -o (G). Thin, lean
ischy, -r, -ro (G). Strong, powerful; hard
=isis (G My). An Egyptian goddess
islandic (NL). Of Iceland
-ism (E). Belief; the process of; an interrelation of organs.
iso (G). Equal
isola (F). An island; alone

-issim, =a, =um, =us (L). (the
  superlative ending)
ist, -o (G). A web; tissue
-ist, -o (G). (the superlative
  ending)
isthm, -o, =us (G). A narrow
  passage
-ite (E). A stone; a fossil
=itea (G). A willow
-ites (G). Belonging to, having to
  do with
=iter (L). A passage, journey
ithagin (G). Genuine
ithy (G). Straight
itin, -o (G). Made of willow
itiner (L). A journey
-itis (G). Inflammation
ity, -o, =s (G). An edge, rim
iul, =us (G). A centipede
-ium (G). Small
ixi, -a, -o (G). Birdlime; mistletoe
ixal, -o (G). Jumping
ixod (G). Like birdlime
ixy, =s (G). The loins, waist
iyn, -g, =x (G). The wryneck

J

jacamar (Br). A kind of bird
jacan (Br). A kind of bird
jact (L). Throw, toss
jacul (L). Throw
=janus (My). Two-faced; a door
japonic (NL). Of Japan
japy, -g, =x (G). The west-northwest wind
jec, -in, -or, =ur (L). The liver
ject (L). Throw
jejun (L). Hunger; dry
jub, =a (L). A mane; a crest
jucund (L). Pleasant
iug, -o, =um (L). A yoke

juglan, =s, -d (L). The walnut
jugul, =um (L). A little yoke; the
  throat; the collarbone
jul, -i, =us (L). A catkin
junc, =us (L). A rush, reed
juven, -il (L). Youth; young
juxta (L). Near to

K

k (see also c and ch)
kairo (G). The right time
kako (G). Bad
kal, -o (G). Beautiful
kaleido (G). With a beautiful form
kali (G). A hut, nest
kapn, -o (G). Smoke
kary, -o (G). A nut; the nucleus
kel (G). A claw
kelaen, -o (G). Black, murky
keli, -d, =s (G). A stain
kelo (G). A hernia, rupture
kelyph, -o (G). A shell, husk
ken, -o (G). New; empty
kentr, -o (G). A point; a spur
=kera, -to (G). Horn
keraun, -o (G). A thunderbolt
kerm, -es (Ps). Crimson
kero (G). Wax
kilo (G). A thousand
kine, -ma, -mato, -s, -si, -t, -to
  (G). Move, moving, movement
kio, -no (G). A pillar; the uvula
klept, -o (G). Steal; a thief
koni, -o (G). Dust
korethr (G). A broom
koro (G). The pupil of the eye
kotyl, -o (G). A cup, socket, cavity
kraur, -o (G). Dry, brittle
kurt, -i, -o (G). Curved
kyan, -o (G). Dark blue
kyll, -o (G). Lame, crippled
kym, -a, -o (G). A wave

kypho, -s (G). Bent
kyrio (G). Master of; critical
kyst, -ho, -o (G). A hollow place;
a cell

L

la, -o (G). A stone; the people
labe (L): A downfall; a defect; (G):
a handle
labell, =um (L). A little lip
labi, -a, -o (L). A lip
labi, -d, =s (G). Forceps
labor (L). Work
labr, -i, -o (L). A lip; a kind of
fish
labra, -c, =x (G). A sea fish
labro (G). Fierce, furious
labyrinth, -o, =us (G). A maze,
labyrinth
lac (L). Milk; a basin; a pit
lacc, -o, =us (G). A cistern, pit
lacca (It). Varnish, wax
lacer, -at (L). Mangled, torn
lacert (L). A lizard; the upper arm
lacertos (L). Strong, powerful
laches, -i (L). Destiny, fate
lachn, -o (G). Woolly
lachr, -im, -ym (L). Tears,
weeping
laci, -d, -st (G). Rent, torn
lacin, -i, =ia (L). A flap
lacm, -u (Dan). Dark violet blue
lacr, -im, -um (L). Tears, weeping
lact, -e, -i, -o (L). Milk
lactis, -m (G). Kick, trample
lactuc, =a (L). Lettuce
lacun, =a (L). A basin, lake; a
space, cavity
lacustr (NL). Of a lake
laelaps (G). A hurricane
laem, -o, =us (G). The throat,
gullet

laemarg, -o (G). Greedy
laen, =a (L). A cloak
laeo (G). The left-hand side
laet (L). Gay, pleasing
laetam, =en, -in (L). Dung
=laetma, -to (G). The depths of the
sea
laev, -i, -o (L). Smooth; nimble,
light; to the left
laevigat (L). Smooth, slippery
lag, -o, =us (G). A hare
lagar, -o (G). Lax, loose
lagen, =a (G). A flask
lagn, -o (G). Lustful, lewd
lago (G). A hare
laguncul, =a (L). A little flask
=lagus (G). A hare
lailaps (G). A hurricane
laim, -o, =us (G). The throat,
gullet
lal, -i, -o (G). Talk, speak
lall (L). Babble
lamb, -a, -en (L). Lick, licking
lambd (G). Like the letter "lambda"
lamell, =a, -i (L). A small plate
lament (L). Wailing
=lamia (G). A vampire-like monster
lamin, =a, -i (L). A thin plate, sheet,
layer
lamn, =a (G). A predaceous fish
lamp, -ad, =as, -s (G). Shine; torch
lampr, -o (G). Brilliant, clear
lampyri, -d, =s (G). A glow worm
lan, =a, -i, -o (L). Wool
lance, =a, -i (L). A lance
lancin (L). Tear, lacerate
langu, -i (L). Weak, faint
languri, =a (L). A lizard
lani (L). Wool
lani, -a, -o (L). A butcher; rend
lanici (L). Woolly
lano (L). Wool

lanth, -an, -o (G). Conceal, lie
  hid, unseen
lanu, -g (L). Wool, down
lao (G). A stone; the people
lapact (G). Empty
lapar, -o (G). The loins; loose
lapath, -i, =um (L). Sorrel, dock
laphyr, =a, -o (G). Booty, spoils
lapi, -d, =s (L). A stone
lapp, =a (L). A bur; burdock
lapponic (L). Of Lapland
laps (L). Slip, glide; a mistake
=lapsana (G). A kind of cress
laque, =us (L). A noose
lar, -i, =us (L). A gull
larc, -o, =us (G). A basket
lari, -c, =x (L). The larch
larin, -o (L). Fat
=larus (L). A gull
larv, =a, -i (L). A ghost, spectre
larvi (NL). A larva
laryn, -g, -go, =x (G). The gullet,
  larynx
lascivi (L). Lewd, wanton; playful,
  sporty
lasi, -o (G). Shaggy, hairy
lass, -it (L). Faint
lat, -i (L). Broad, wide
lata, -g, =x (G). A beaver; a drop
  of wine
latebr, =a, -i (L). A hiding place
laten, -t (L). Hidden, hiding
later, -al, -o (L). The side
lateri (L). The side; a brick
lateri, -ci, -ti (L). Made of brick
latesc (L). Becoming hidden
=latex (L). A liquid, fluid
lathri, -di, -o (G). Hidden, secret
lathyr, =us (G). A kind of vetch
lati (L). Broad, wide
latic, -i (L). A liquid, fluid
latr, =y (G). Worship, serve

latra, -n, -t (L). Bark; barking
latri (G): A servant; (L): wash
latro (G): Pay, hire; a hireling; (L):
  a robber
-latry (G). Worship, serve
=latus (L). The side; broad, wide
lauda (L). Praise
laur, -eat, -i, =us (L). The laurel
=laura (G). An alley
laut (L). Washed, elegant, noble
lava, -t (L). Wash, bathe
lax, -a, -i (L). Loose, loosen
lazul (LL). Azure, blue
leberi, -d, =s (G). A snakeskin
lecan, =a (G). A dish, pan
lech, -o (G). A lying-in woman; a
  bed
lechri, -o (G). Slanting, oblique
leci, -d, =s (G). A little plate
lecith, -o (G). The yolk of an egg
lect (G): Chosen, picked; (L): a
  bed; a gathering
lect, -icul, -ul (L). A couch, bed
lecyth, -o (G). An oil flask
leg, -a, -i (L). Law
leg, -o, =us (G): Lie down; choose;
  (L): collect
legib (LL). Read
legitim (L). Lawful
lego (G). Lie down; choose
legum, =en, -in (L). A legume
=legus (G): Lie down; choose; (L):
  collect
lei, -o (G). Smooth
leich, -o (G). Lick, lap
leima, -c, =x (G). A slug; a garden
leio (G). Smooth; the left-hand side
leip, -o (G). Leave; lack
leir, -o (G). Pale
leist, -o (G). Plundering
lem, -i, -o (G). A pestilence, plague
=lemma, -to (G). A husk, peel, sheath

=lemna (G). A water plant
lemnisc, =us (L). A ribbon
lemo (G). The throat; a plague
=lemon, -i (L). A meadow
lemur (L). A ghost, spirit
len, =s, -t (L). A lentil, bean
leni, -en (L). Soft, mild
leno (G). Wool
lent (L). Thick, sticky, slow
lenti (L). A lentil, bean
lentig, -inos (L). Freckled
leo, -ni, -nt (L G). A lion
lepa, -d, =s (G). A shellfish, limpet
lepi, -do, =s, -sma (G). A scale
lepist, =a (L). A goblet
lepo (G). A husk, scale
lepor, -i (L). A hare
lepr, -a, -o (G). Scaly; leprosy
leps, =is (G). A seizure
lept, -ale, -ino, -o (G). Fine, slender
=leptes (G). A receiver
=lepus (L). A hare
lepyr, -o, =um (G). A shell, husk
lere, -m, -si (G). Idle talk
lesi (L). Hurt
lest, =es, -ic, -r (G). A robber, pirate
leth, -arh, -i, -o (G). Forgetfulness, oblivion
leuc, -o (G). White
leucani (G). The throat
leucom, =a (G). Whiteness
leuk, -o (G). White
leur, -o (G). Smooth, even
leva (L). Raise, lift up
levator (L). A lifter
levi (L). Smooth; light
levigat (L). Polished
levo (L). The left-hand side
lexi (G). Cessation; a word, speech

liban, -o, =us (G). Incense
libat (L). Pour
libell, =a (L). A level
libell, =us (L). A book, pamphlet
liber (L). Free; the inner bark; a book; a child
libera, -l, -t (L). Free
liberi (L). A child
libid (L). Desire, passion
libo (G). Tears
=libra (L). A balance, scales
librar, -i (L). Of books
libri (L). A book; the inner bark
licha (G). The space between the thumb and first finger; a steep cliff
lichan (G). Licking; the forefinger
=lichen, -i, -o (G). A lichen
lichn, -o (G). Dainty; greedy
=lien, -i, -o (L). The spleen
liga, -m, -t (L). Bound, tied; a band
lign, -e, -i, =um (L). Wood
lignyot (L). Smoky, sooty
ligul, =a (L). A shoe tongue, strap
ligustr, =um (L). Privet
ligy, -r, -ro (G). Clear, loud
lili, =um (L). A lily
lim (L). Mud, slime; looking sideways
lim, =a, -o (L). A file
lima, -c, =x (L). A snail, slug
liman (NL). Mud, slime
limat (L). Polished
limb, =us (L). An edge; a head band
=limen (L). A threshold
limer, -o (G). Hungry
limi (L). Mud, slime
limin (L). A threshold
limit (L). A boundary
=limma, -to (G). A remnant
limn, =a, -i, -o (G). A marsh; a lake

limo (G): Hunger; a meadow; (L): a file
=limon (G). A meadow
=limonium (G). Sea lavender
limos (L). Muddy
limpid (L). Clear
=limus (L). Mud
lin, -a, -ar, -o, =um (L). Flax
lin, -ea, -eo, -o (L). A line
lin, -o, =um (G). A net, cloth
linct (L). Licked
lingu, =a (L). The tongue
lini, -m, -t (L). Smear
lino (L): A line; flax; (G): a net, cloth
linol (L). Flax oil
=linum (L): Flax; (G): a net, cloth
linyph (G). Weaving linen
lio, -t (G). Smooth; smoothness
lip, -o (G). Fat; lack; leave
lipar (G). Oily, fatty; perseverance
liphem (G). Lacking blood
lipp, -i (L). Bleary-eyed, dim-sighted
lips (G). Leaving
lipsan, -o, =um (G). A relic, remnant
lipsi, =a (G). An omission
liqu, -e, -i (L). Fluid, liquid
lir, =a (L). A ridge
liri, -o, =um (G). A lily
liro (G). Pale; bold
liss, -a, -o (G). Smooth
listr, -io, -o, =um (G). A spade
-lite (G). A stone
litera (L). A letter
lith, -io, -o, =us (G). A stone
litig, -i (L). A dispute
lito (G). Smooth
liter, -a, -e, -i (L). The seashore
litr, -a (G). A pound

littor, -a, -e, -i (L). The seashore
litu, =us (L). A crook, augur's staff
litur (L). Erase
liv, -e, -id (L). Ashen, bluish
lixivi (L). Ash-colored; lye
lob, -i, -o, =us (G). A lobe
lobat (NL). Lobed
loc, -a, -o, =us (L). A place
loch, -o, =us (G). An ambush
lochi, =a, -o (G). Childbirth, confinement
lochm, =a (G). A thicket
locul, =us (L). A little place, cell
locust, =a, -i (L). A locust, grasshopper
lodi, -c, =x (L). A blanket
loem, -o, =us (G). A plague
log, -o, =us, =y (G). A word, discourse, study of
loga, -do, =s (G). The conjunctivae; the whites of the eyes; picked, chosen
loim, -o, =us (G). A plague
lolig, -in, =o (L). A squid, cuttlefish
=lolium (L). The darnell
=loma, -to (G). A hem, fringe
loment, =um (L). A cosmetic, wash; bean meal
lomvia (Far). The murre
lonch, =a, -o (G). A spear, lance
long, -i (L). Long
lop, -ism, -o, =us (G). A scale; husk
loph, -i, -o, =us (G). A crest, tuft
loquac (L). Talkative
lor, =um (L). A thong, lash
lord, -o (G). Bent backward
lori (Mal). A kind of parrot
=lorica (L). Clothed in metal; armor, breastplate
=lorum (L). A thong, lash
lot, -io, =us (L). A washing

lot, -o, =us (G). The lotus
lox, -o (G). Slanting, oblique
lubric (L). Smooth, slippery
luc, -i (L). Light; a grove
lucan (LL). A kind of beetle
lucern, =a (L). A lamp
luci, -d (L). Light; clear, shining
luci, -o, =us (L). The pike
luco (G). A wolf
lucr (L). Gain, profit
luct (L). Struggle, wrestle
luctuos (L). Mournful, sorrowful
=lucus (L). A grove; a light
lud, -i, -icr (L). Play
ludovician (NL). Of Louisiana
lue, =s (L). A plague
lugubr (L). Sad, gloomy
lumac (It). A snail
lumb, -a, -o, =us (L). The loin
lumbric, -i, =us (L). An earth-
worm
=lumen, lumin (L). Light
lun, =a, -i (L). The moon
lunul, =a (L). A crescent
lup, -i, -o, =us (L). A wolf
lupin, -o (L). A lupine; of a wolf
lupul, =us (L). The hop plant
=lura (L). The mouth of a bag
lurid (L). Pale, ghastly, wan
lusc (L). One-eyed
luscini, =a (L). The nightingale
lusitanic (L). Of Portugal
lustr (L). Shining, pure, washed
lut, -e, -i (L). Mud; mud-colored,
yellowish
lutr, -o (G). A bath, bathing
lutr, =a (L). An otter
=lux (L). Light
luxa, -t (L). Displace, dislocate
luxur, -i (L). Extravagance, splendor
ly, -o (G). Loose

lyc, -o, =us (G). A wolf
lychn, =is (G). A kind of plant
lychn, -o, =us (G). A lamp
lycos (G). A kind of spider
lygae (G). Gloomy
lygi (G). Twilight; bend
lygi, -sm (G). Bend; bending
lygm (G). Hiccough
lygo (G). A twig, a pliant rod
lygr, -o (G). Cowardly; mournful
=lyma (G). Destruction; filth
lymph, =a, -o (L). Water; a water
nymph
lymphat, -i, -o (L). Frantic; lymph
lyn, -c, =x (G). A lynx; hiccough
lyo (G). Loose
lyp, -e, -ero, -o (G). Pain, dis-
tress; painful
lypr, -o (G). Wretched
lyr, =a, -i (G). A harp, lyre
lys, -i, =is, -io (G). Loose; a
loosening
lyss, =a, -o (G). Madness, rage
lyt, -o (G). That which may be
loosed
lythr, -o, =um (G). Blood, gore
lytt, =a (G). Madness, rage; a
worm thought to cause madness in
dogs

M

macar, -i, -o (G). Blessed, happy
macell, =a (G). A pick axe
macer, -a (L). Soften
mach, -a, -i, -o (G). Fight
macha, -er, -ir (G). A sword,
dagger, razor
machin, =a (L). An engine, machine
maci, -a (L). Leanness
macr, -o (G). Large, long
mactr, =a, -i (G). A kneading trough
=macula, -t (L). Spot; spotted

mad, -e, -id (L). Wet
mad, -o (G). Barley bread
madar, -o (G). Bald; flaccid
madre (Sp). Mother
meandr (G). Winding, zigzag
maeeu, -si, -sio (G). Childbirth
maen, -a, -ad, ⸗as (G). Rave;
  excited
maen, ⸗a, -i (G). A herring
magist, ⸗er, -r (L). A teacher,
  master
⸗magma (G). A mass
magn, -i (L). Great, large
magne, -to (G). A magnet
mai, ⸗a, -o (G). A kind of crab
maieu, -si, -sio (G). Childbirth
maior (L). Larger
maira (G). Shine, sparkle
major (L). Larger
makr, -o (G). Large, long
mal, ⸗a (L). The jaw, cheek
mal, -e, -i, -ign (L). Bad, evil,
  wrong; imperfect; not
mal, -i, ⸗us (L). An apple
mal, -o (G). Woolly, soft
malac, -h, -i, -o (G). Soft
malari (It). Bad air
male (L). Bad, evil, wrong
malell, ⸗a (L). A little jaw
mali (L). Bad, evil, wrong; an
  apple
maliasm, ⸗us (G). A skin disease
malign (L). Bad, evil, wrong
mall, -o, ⸗us (G). Wool
malle, ⸗us (L). A hammer
malo (G). Woolly, soft
malt, -o (G). Malt
malth, -a, -aco, -e, -o (G). A soft
  wax; pliant
⸗malus (L). An apple; bad, evil,
  wrong
malv, ⸗a (L). The mallow

mamill, ⸗a (L). A teat
mamm, ⸗a, -i, -il (L). A teat
mammal, -i (L). A mammal
man, -o (G). Wide, roomy
man, -u (L). A hand
manat (Sp). The manatee
manc (L). Maimed
mancip (L). A purchaser
-mancy (G). Divination
mand (L). Order; chew
manda (L). Order
mandibul (L). A jaw
⸗mandra (G). A stable
mandragor (G). The mandrake
manduc (L). Chew
⸗manes (G). A cup; a slave
mang, -i (Pg). The mango
mani, ⸗a (G). Rage, madness
manicat (L). With long sleeves
manipul (L). A handful
mann, -o, ⸗us (G). A collar, necklace
mano (G). Rare, thin, roomy
mant (Sp). A mantle, cloak
mantell, ⸗um (L). A cloak
manti, -d, ⸗s (G). A soothsayer; a
  kind of grasshopper
mantill (Sp). A light cloak
mantisp (L). Mantid-like
mantiss, ⸗a (L). A small addition
manu, ⸗s (L). A hand
manubri, ⸗um (L). A handle
mar, -i (L). The sea
marant (G). Wither, waste
marasm (G). Waste, decay
marc, ⸗us (L). A hammer
marc, -esc, -id (L). Withering
marg, -in, ⸗o (L). A border, edge
margarit, ⸗es (G). A pearl
mari (L). The sea; male
marian (NL). Of Mary
marin (L). Of the sea, marine
maring, -o (G). The eardrum

marit, -a (L). A husband
maritim (L). Of the sea, marine
marma, -r (G). Marble; sparkle, glisten
=marmor, -i (L). Marble
marpt, -o (G). Seize
marrubi, =um (L). Hoarhound
mars, -ipo, -upi (G). A bag, pouch
marti (L). Mars, god of war
=mas (L). Male
masar (NL). Stick out the lip
maschal (G). The armpits
mascul, -in (L). Male, masculine
masesi (G). Chewing
mass, -a, -o (G). Knead; larger
=masseter (G). A chewer
massul, =a (L). A little mass
mast, -o, =us (G). A breast, nipple
masta, -c, =x (G). The mouth, jaws
mastic (L). Chew
mastig, -o, =mastix (G). A whip
masto (G). A breast, nipple
masturba (L). Pollute one's-self
=mastus (G). A breast, nipple
mat, -aeo, -eo (G). Foolish, idle
=mater, -n (L). A mother
math (G). Learn
matr, -i, -o (L). A mother
matri, -c, =x (L). A place where something is generated; the womb, uterus
matron, =a (L). A wife
matt (L). A mat; dull-colored
matur (L). Ripe; ripen
matutin (L). The morning
maur, -o (G). Dark, obscure
maxill, =a, -i (L). The jaw, jawbone
maxim (L). Largest, greatest
maz, -ia, -o (L). The breast; a cake
me (G). Not

meandr (L). Winding, twisting
meat, =us (L). A passage
mechan, -i, -o (G). An instrument, machine
mecist, -o (G). Longest
meco (G). Long; length
mecon, -i, -o (G). The poppy; opium; the ink bag of a cuttlefish; the fecal matter discharged by a newborn child
mecyn, -o (G). Extend, prolong
mede, =a (G). The genitals
medeol (L My). Medea, a sorceress
medi, -a, -o (L). The middle
medic, -a, -o (L). Heal; healing
medo (G). A bladder; a guardian
medull, =a (L). Marrow, pith
medus, =a, -i (L My). A jellyfish
meg, -a, -alo (G). Large, great
megar, -on, =um (G). A large room
megist, -o (G). Largest, greatest
mei, -o (G). Less
meiz, -o (G). Larger, greater
mel, =a, -o (G). The cheeks
mel, -i, -it, -ito (G). Honey
mel, -o (G). A song; a limb; an apple
melaen (G). Black; blacken
melan, -o (G). Black
=melas (G). Black, dark
meldo (G). Melt
meleagri, =s (G). A guinea fowl
=meles (L). A badger
meli, -d, -n (L). A badger
meli, -t, -to (G). Honey
=melia (G). An ash tree
melichr, -o (G). Honey-colored
melid (L). A badger
melin (G): The quince; ashen; (L): a badger
melior (L). Better

melism (G). A song; a dismem-
  bering
meliss, =a (G). A honey bee; honey
melit, -o (G). Honey
melizo (G). Sing
mell, -i, -it (L). Honey
melo (G). A limb; the cheeks; a
  probe; a song; an apple, fruit; a
  sheep
melod, -i (G). Song, a singing
meloe, meloi (G). A probe
melolonth, =a (G). A cockchafer
melon (G). An apple, fruit; a
  sheep
melos (G). Probing
melotri, -di (G). Probe, sound
melyr, =is (G). A song-maker; a
  kind of insect
memat, -o (G). Desired
membra, -c, =x (G). A kind of
  insect
membran, =a (L). A membrane
memnoni (L). Brownish black
=men, -o (G). A month
mena, -do (G). The moon
menda, -c, =x (L). Lying, false
mendic (L). Poor; a beggar
mene (G). The menses; the moon
meni (G). Anger; the moon; a
  month
menin, -g, -go, =x (G). A membrane
menisc, -o (G). A crescent
meno (G). Remain, stand fast; a
  month; the menses
mens (L). The mind; measure
mens, =a (L). A table
mens, -e, -i (L). A month
menstru (L). Monthly
mensur (L). Measure
ment, -a, -i (L). The mind

ment, -i, =um (L). The chin
menth, =a (L). Mint
mentul, =a (L). The penis
meny (G). Inform, reveal
mephit, -i, =is (L). A foul odor
mer (L). Pure; alone; bare
mer, =e, -i, -o (G). A part; the
  thigh
mercur (L My). Mercury, a Grecian
  god
merd, =a, -i (L). Dung, excrement
mere, -t (L). Earn
merg (L). Dive, dip
=mergus (L). A diver
meri, -d, =s (G). A part
meriae (G). Of the thigh
meridi (L). Noon
meridional (L). Southern
merism, -o, =us (G). A division
merist, -o (G). Divided
merit (L). Earn
merluci, =us (NL). A kind of fish
mermi, =s, -th (G). A cord
mero (G). A part; the thigh
merop, -o, =s (G). The bee-eater
-merous (G). Parted
mers (L). Dip
merul, =a (L). A blackbird
=merus (G). The thigh
meryc, -o (G). Ruminate, chew the
  cud
mes, -o (G). The middle
mesa (Sp). Table land
mesar, -a, -i, =um (G). A mesen-
  tery
mesat (G). Middle, median
mesembri, =a (G). Noon
mesit, =es (G). A mediator
meso (G). The middle
mesotoech, -o (G). A dividing wall
mest, -o (G). Full

met, -a, -h (G). Between, with, after, back again; change

=meta (L). A boundary; a turning post

metab, -as, -ol (G). Change

metall, -i, -o (G). Mine; metal

metallurg (G). Metal-working

metax, -i, -y (G). Between

meteor, -o (G). High in the air; heavenly bodies; natural phenomena, the weather

=meter (G). Measure

meth (G). Between, with, after, back again; change

meth, -e, -o, -y (G). Drink, drunkenness; wine

method, -o (G). A system

methys (G). Intoxicated, drunk

metop, -i, -o (G). The forehead

metr, -a, -i, -o (G). Measure; the uterus, womb; a mother

metrio (G). Moderately

-metry (G). Measurement

=meum (L). A kind of plant

mezzo (It). The middle; half

miar, -o (G). Defiled, stained with blood

miasm, =a, -o (G). Pollution

=mica, -r (L). A crumb

micace (L). Granular

micell, =a (L). A little crumb

micr, -o (G). Small

mict, -o (G). Mixed

mictur (L). Urinate

mid (ME). The middle

mida, =s (G). A kind of insect

migr, -a (L). Wander, migrate

migratori (L). Wandering, migratory

mili, -ar, -ol, =um (L). Millet

milit, -ar, -i (L). A soldier

mill, -e, -i, -o (L). One thousand

milph, -o (G). Bald; losing hair

milt, -o (G). Ochre; red, vermilion

milv, -in, =us (L). A kite

mim, -e, -i, -o, =us (G). An imitation; an actor, mimic

mina, -c, =x (L). A threat; project

minera (ML). Mine

mineral, -o (ML). Mineral

mini, -a, =um (L). Red lead

minim (L). Least, smallest

minor (L). Less, smaller; hang over, threaten

minus (L). Less, smaller

minut (L). Small

miny, -th, =s (G). Small

minyr, -o (G). Complaining

minyth (G). Small; decrease

mio (G). Less

mir, -a, -ab, -ac, -i (L). Wonderful

mis (E): Wrong; (G): hate

misc (L). Mix; mixed

misc, -o (G). A stalk

misch, -o, =us (G). A stalk

mise, -ll, -r (L). Wretched

miso (G). Hate, hatred

miss, -i (L). Send

mist, =us (L). A mixing

mist, -o (G). Most

-mit (L). Send

mit, -o, =us (G). A thread

mitell, =a (L). A head band

miter (L). A cap

miti (L). Mild, harmless; ripe

mitig (L). Make mild

mito (G). A thread

mitr, =a, -i (L). A cap, turban

=mitus (G). A thread

mix, -i, -o (G). Mix

mnem, -at, -on (G). Memory; remember

mni, -o, =um (G). Moss
mobil (L). Movable
mochl, -o, =us (G). A lever
mochth, -o, =us (G). Hard work
mod, -u (L). Measure
modena (N). Deep purple
modic (L). Moderate
modiol, =us (L). A small measure;
 a bucket on a water wheel
modul (L). Measure; a tune
moell (F). Pith, marrow
moen, -i (L). Walls, fortifications
moer, =a, -o (G). Lot, fate; a part,
 division
moest (L). Sorrowful, sad
mog, -i, -o (G). Hardly, with difficulty; trouble
moir, -a, -o (G). Lot, fate; a part,
 division
mol, -i (G). Hardly, with difficulty
mola, -r (L). Grind, mill
molecul (L). A little mass
molest (L). Disturb
molen (L). Grinding
molg, -o (G). Hide, skin
molge (Ger). A salamander
moli (G). Hardly, with difficulty
molin, =a (L). A mill
moll, -i (L). Soft
mollusc (L). Soft; a shellfish
molop, -o, =s (G). A ridge, weal,
 bruise
=molothrus (L). An intruder
molp (G). A song
molpast, =es (G). A dancer
molybd, -i, -o (G). Lead
molyn, -a (G). Stain, defile
molysm, -o (G). Pollution
=momentum (L). Motion
momo, -s, =us (G). Blame, disgrace
momot (from its cry). The motmot

mon, -a, -er, -o (G). One, single
monet (L). Money; mint
monil, -i (L). A necklace, string
 of beads
monimo (G). Fixed, steadfast
monit (L). Warn; warning
mono (G). One, single
monstr, -a (L). Show, warn; a
 monster
mont, -an, -i (L). A mountain
mor, -i, =us (L). A mulberry
mor, -o (G). Stupid, foolish
mora, -tor (L). Delay
morb, -i, -os (L). A disease; diseased
morbill (ML). The measles
morchel (Ger). A morel
mord, -ac, -ax, -el, -en, -ic (L).
 Bite, biting
mori (L): A mulberry; (G) folly
moribund (L). Dying
morill (F). A fungus, morel
morind, =a (L). A mulberry
morinell (G). Foolish
morio (G). A part; a fool; a nar-
 cotic plant
=mormo (G). A monster, bugbear
mormyr, -o, =us (G). A sea fish
moro (G). Stupid, foolish
moros (L). Fretful
morph, =a, -o (G). Form
morph, -e, -o (L My). Sleep
morrhu, =a (L). The cod fish
mors (L). Bite, biting, eat
mort, al, -i, -u (L). Death, dead, deadly
morul, =a (L). A little mulberry
=morus (L). A mulberry
mosch, -o, =us (G). Musk; a young
 animal
mot, -a, -i, -o (L). Move; motion
motacill, =a (L). The wagtail

muc, -e, -i, -o, =us (L). Mold,
moldy; mucus
=mucro, -n (L). A sharp point
=mugil, -i (L). The mullet
mulc (L). Stroke, caress
mulg (L). To milk
mulin (L). Of a mule
mull, =us (L). The red mullet
mulo (L). A mule
muls, -i (L). Mixed with honey,
sweet
mult, -i (L). Many
mund, -an (L). The world;
adorned; clear
mur (L). A mouse; a wall
mura (L). A wall
muraen, =a (L). A lamprey, eel
=murex (L). The purple-fish; purple
muri (L). A mouse; a wall
=muria (L). Brine
muric (L). The purple-fish; purple
muricat (L). Pointed
muricul (L). Slightly pointed
murin (L). Of a mouse
=mus (L). A mouse
mus, -a, -o (Ar). The banana
musc, -a, -i, -o (L). A fly; moss;
musk
muscari (L). Of a fly; a clothes
brush
muscid (L). Mossy
muscul, -o, =us (L). Muscle; a little
mouse; a kind of fish
=muscus (L). Moss; musk
museo (L). A museum
musi (G). Music; a muse
music, -o (G). Music
muso (Ar). A banana
muss (L). Mutter, buzz
must (L). Fresh; new wine
mustel, =a, -in (L). A weasel
mut (L). Dumb

muta (L). Change
muti, -c, -l (L). Cut off
mutu (L). Reciprocal; borrowed
my, -i, =ia (G). A fly
my, -o, =s (G). A muscle; a mouse
mya, -c, =x (G). A sea mussel
myagr, =um (G). A mouse trap
=myaria (G). Muscle
myc, -e, -et, -eto, -o (G). A fungus
=mycetes (G). The bellflower
mych, -o (G). Inward
myct, =er, -ir (G). The nose
myd, -a, -ale, -o (G). Wet, damp;
moldy
mydr, -o, =us (G). A red-hot mass
mydriasi, =s (G). A dilation of the
pupil
myel, -o, =us (G). Marrow; the
spinal cord
mygal, =e (L). A field mouse
myi, =a, -o (G). A fly
myl, -io, -o (G). A mill, millstone;
a molar
mylabr, =is (G). An insect in flour
mills
mylacr, =is (G). A millstone
myll, -o, =us (G). A lip; crooked; a
salted sea fish
mymar (G). Ridicule; blame
myo (G). A muscle; a mouse
myop, =s (G). Short-sighted; a
horse fly
myosot (G). Mouse-eared
myox, =us (G). A dormouse
myr, -o, =um (G). Ointment, perfume
myrc (NL). The myrtle
myri, -a, -o (G). Numberless;
10,000
myri, -st (G). Anoint
myric, =a (G). The tamarask
myrin, -g, -go, =x (NL). The eardrum

myrio (G). Numberless; 10,000
myrist (G). Anoint; ointment
myrme, -co, =x (G). An ant
myro (G). Ointment, perfume
myrsin, =a (G). The myrtle
myrt, =us (G). The myrtle
=myrum (G). Ointment, perfume
=mys (G). A muscle; a mouse
mysi, =s (G). A closing of the
    lips or eyes
myso (G). Filth, abomination
myst, -ac, =ax, -ic (G). The
    upper lip; a moustache
myst, -eri, -i, -o (G). A mystery,
    secret rite
mystr, -i, -io, =ium, -o (G). A
    spoon
myth, -o, =us (G). A legend
mytil, -o, =us (G). A mussel
myx, =a, -o (G). Slime, mucus,
    nasal discharge
myxin, =us (G). A slime fish
myz, -o (G). Suck; mutter

N

nabi, -d, =s (L). A giraffe
=nabla (G). A kind of harp
nacr (F). Mother-of-pearl
naev, =us (L). A birthmark, mole,
    spot
naia, -d, =s (G). A water nymph
naid; =nais (G). A water nymph
naj, =a, -i (H). A snake
=nama, -to (G). A stream
nan, -i, -no, -o, =us (G). A
    dwarf
nao (G). A temple
nap, =aea, -o (G). A glen, wooded
    dell
nap, -i, =us (L). A turnip
naphth (G). Asphalt
narc, =a, -o (G). Numbness, stupor

nard, -o, =us (G). The spikenard
nari, =s (L). A nostril
narra (L). Tell
narthe, -c, =x (G). A kind of plant
nas, -i, -o, =us (L). The nose
nasc (L). Birth; be born
nasm, -o, =us (G). A stream
nass, =a (L). A wicker basket
nast, -o (G). Pressed close, solid
=nastes (G). An occupant
nasut (L). Large-nosed
nat, -i, =is (L). The rump, buttocks
nata (L). Birth; be born
natan, -t (L). Swimming
nato (L). Swimming
natri, -c, =x (L). A water snake
nau, =s, -t (G). A ship; sail
nauc, =um (L). Trivial; a trifle
naupli, =us (G). A kind of mollusc
naus, -e, -i (G). Seasickness
naut, -i (G). A ship; sail
nautil, =us (G). A sailor; a shell-
    fish
nav, -a, -i (L). A ship; sail
navicul, =a (L). A little ship, boat
navig, -a (L). Sail, go by ship
ne (G). Not
ne, -o (G). New; swim;. go
neal, =es (G). Young, fresh
nebr, -i, -o, =us (G). A fawn
nebul, =a, -o (L). A cloud, mist
necan, -t (L). Killing
=necator (L). A killer
necr, -o, =us (G). The dead; a dead
    body
necros, =is (G). Death, deadness
nect (L). Bound, joined
nect, -er, -o (G). Swimming
=nectar (G). The drink of the gods
nectri (G). A swimmer
necy, =s (G). A corpse
necydal, =us (G). The silkworm
    larva

nedym, -o (G). Sweet, delightful

neel, -y, =yx (G). A newcomer

nega (L). Deny

negr, -i (Sp). Black

neil, -o (G). Of the Nile

nel, -eo, -i (G). Merciless

nelip, -o (G). Barefooted

nem, =a, -ato, -o (G). A thread

nemerte (G). Unerring

nemor, -al (L). A grove, woodland

neo (G). New, recent; a temple;
swim; go

neo, -ss, -ssi, -tt, -tti, -tto (G).
A bird's nest; a young bird

neochm, -o (G). Make new

nep, =a (L). A scorpion

nepenth, =es (G). Free from
sorrow

nepet, =a (L). A kind of mint

neph, -el, -eli, -elo, -o (G). A
cloud, clouds

nephali (G). Sober, without wine

nephr, -i, -o, =us (G). The kidney

nephthy, =s (G). An Egyptian
goddess

nepot (L). A descendant; extrava-
gant

nepti, =s (L). A granddaughter

neptun, =us (L). A sea god

nere, -i, =is, -o (G). A sea nymph

nerein, -e, -i (L). A sea god

nerit, =es (G). A sea mussel

neri, =um (G). The oleander

nero (G). Wet, liquid

nerv, =us (L). A nerve, tendon

nes, -o, =us (G). An island

nesc (L). Ignorant

=nessa (G). A duck

nest, -i, -o (G). Fasting, hungry

=nestor (L My). Wise

netr, -o, =um (G). A spindle

nett, =a, =ion (G). A duck

neur, =a, -o (G). A nerve, sinew,
cord

neurode (G). Nerve-like; the retina

neust, -o (G). Swim

neutr (L). Neither

nex, =us (L). A tie, bond

nexi (G). Swimming

nexil (L). Tied together

nic, -o (G). Victory; strife

nictitat (L). Winking

nid, -i, =us (L). A nest

nig, -el, =er, -ra, -resc, -ri, -ro (L).
Black, dark

nik, -o (G). Victory; strife

nilo, -tic (L). The Nile; a canal,
aqueduct

nimb, =us (L). A rain cloud

nimr (Hb). A hunter

niph, =a, -o (G). Snow

nipt, -o (G). Wash

=nipter (G). A wash basin

nitid (L). Shining, handsome

nitr, -a, -i, -o (G). Soda; nitrogen

niv, -al, -e, -os (L). Snowy

niv, -i, -o (L). Snow

nobil (L). Well known

noc, -en, -i, -u (L). Harm; harmful

noct, -i (L). Night

noctu, =a (L). A night owl

nod, -i, -o, =us (L). A knot, swelling

nod, -o (G). Toothless

nodul, =us (L). A little knot

noe, -a (G). Think

=noema, -to (G). A thought

noetic, -o (G). Intelligent

noia (G). The mind

nol, =a, -i (LL). A small bell

nom, -o (G). A pasture; custom, law

nom, =en, -in (L). A name

noma, -d (G). Roving, spreading

nome (G). A shepherd; a feeding

nomi, -co, -si, -o (G). Law, custom

nomo (G). A pasture; custom, law

-nomy (G). The science of

non (L). Not; the ninth

nonagen (L). Ninety

noo, -s (G). The mind

nop, -o (G). Blind

norm, =a (L). A rule, measure

nosazonto (G). Fall ill

nose, -m; noso (G). Disease, sickness

nost, -a, -o (G). Return home

nostoc (Ger). A kind of alga

not, -a, -ae, -al, -o, =um (G). The back

not, -o (G). The south wind; the south

notat (L). Marked

note, -o (G). South, southwest

noter, -o (G). Damp, moist

noth, -o (G). Spurious, illegitimate

nothr, -o (G). Sluggish

noti, -o (G). Wet, moist; southern

notidan, -o (G). Having a pointed dorsal fin

noto (G). The back; south, southwest

notor (L). Known, making known

=notum (G). The back

nous (G). The mind

nov, -i, -o (L). New

novaboracens (L). Of New York

novem (L). Nine

noverc, =a (L). A stepmother

novi, novo (L). New

noxi, -os (L). Harmful

nub, -a (L). Marry

nub, -e, -i (L). A cloud

nuc, -ell, -i (L). A nut

nuch, =a (ML). The nape

nucle, -a, -i, -o (L). A little nut; the nucleus

nucleol, =us (L). A little nucleus

nud, -i (L). Nude, naked

nuga, -t (L). Joke, jest

nulli (L). No, none

numeni (G). A curlew; the new moon

numer (L). Number

numid (L). Roving, wandering

=numisma, -t (L). A coin

nummul, =us (L). Money

nun, -ci, -ti (L). A messenger

=nuphar (G). A water lily

nupt, -ial (L). Marry; a wedding

nut, -a, -an (L). Nod, nodding, sway

nutri (L). Feed, nourish

nutri, -c, =x (L). A nurse

=nux (L). A nut

nyc, -t, -ti, -to (G). Night

nycter, -i (G). A bat

=nygma, -to (G). A puncture wound

-nym (G). A name

nymph, =a (G). A nymph; a bride

nymphae, =a (G). A water lily

nyroc, =a (NL). A merganser

nyss, =a (L My). A water nymph; a starting post

nyss, -o (G). Prick, stab

nysta, -gm (G). Nodding the head, drowsy

=nyx (G). Night

nyx, -eo, =is (G). A puncture

O

o, -o (G). An egg

oari, -o· (G). A small egg; a mate, wife

=oasis (G). A fertile spot

ob (L). Reversed, against

obdur (L). Harden

obel, -isc (G). A spit, pointed pillar; a round cake

=obex (L). A barrier
obfuscat (L). Darkened
obic (L). A barrier
obit, =us (L). Death; an approach
oblat (L). Spread out
oblig (L). Bound, obliged; bind
obliqu (L). Oblique
oblitera (L). Erase
oblivi (L). Forget
obnoxi (L). Hazardous; liable
obnubil (L). Clouded, covered
obol, -o (G). A coin
obri, =a, -o (G). The young of
  animals
obscur (L). Covered, dark
obsole, -sc, -t (L). Decayed,
  worn out
obstetri, -c, =x (L). A midwife
obstru (L). Close up, block
obtect (L). Concealed, covered
obtur (L). Close, stop up
obtus (L). Dull, blunt
oc (L). Reversed, against
occiden, -tal (L). Western
occip, -it, =ut (L). The back of
  the head, occiput
occlu, -d, -s (L). Shut up
occult (L). Hidden
ocean, -o (G). The ocean
oceanit, =es (G). An ocean
  dweller
ocell, =us (L). A little eye
ocelo (Mex). An ocelot
och, -o, =us (G). Anything that
  holds or supports
=ochema, -to (G). A support; a carriage; a vessel
ocher (G). Pale
ochet, -o, =us (G). A drain
ochl, -o, =us (G). A crowd, mob
ochn, =a (G). A pear tree
ocho (G). Anything that holds or
  supports

ochr, -o (G). Pale; pale yellow
ochth, =a, -o (G). A hill
=ochus (G). Anything that holds or
  supports
ochyr, -o (G). Stout, firm
-ocl (L). An eye
ocn, -o (G). Inactive; hesitating
ocr, -i (G). Pale; a ridge, summit
ocre, =a (L). A legging
oct, -i, -o (L). Eight
ocul, -i, -o, =us (L). An eye
ocy (G). Swift
-od (NL). Form
od, -e, -o, =us (G). A way
-oda (G). Like; a resemblance
oda, -c, =x (G). Biting
ode (G). A song; a way; like
odeon (G). A song
-odes (G). Like
odi (G): A song; (L): hate
odin, -o (G). Labor pain
odo (G). A way; swollen
odon, -t, -to (G). A tooth
=odor, -i (L). An odor, smell
=odus (G). A way
odyn, =e, =ia, -o (G). Pain
oe (see also ae, ai, or e)
oec, -i, -o, =us (G). A house,
  dwelling
=oecetes (G). An inhabitant
oed, -e, =ema, -o (G). A swelling,
  tumor
oeg, -o (G). Open
oem, -a, -o (G). A way, path
oen, -a (G). A wild pigeon
oen, -o, =us (G). Wine
oenanth (G). The first shoot of the
  vine; the windflower; a small bird
oesophag, -i, -o (G). The gullet,
  esophagus
oestr, -o, =us (G). A gadfly; sting;
  frenzy
ogdoa (G). Eight

ogm, -o, =us (G). A furrow
ogyg (G My). A king of Athens
oico (G). A house, dwelling
-oid (G). Like; form
oide, =ma (G). A swelling, tumor
-oidea (the ending of animal super-
  family names)
-oideae (the ending of plant subfamily names)
oidi (G). A small egg
oido (G). A swelling, tumor
oig, -o (G). Open
oik, -o, =us (G). A house, dwelling
ol, -o (G). Whole, entire
olbi, -o (G). Blessed, happy
ole, =a, -astr (L). An olive; an
  olive tree
ole, -i, -o, =um (L). Olive oil,
  oil
ole, -nt, -o (L). Emit a smell,
  smell
oleagin (L). Olive-shaped
olear (L). Oily, of oil
olecran, -o, =um (G). The elbow
olei (L). Oil, olive oil
olen, =a, -e, -i (G). The elbow
olen, -t (L). Emit a smell, smell
oleo (L). Oil, olive oil; emit a
  smell, smell
oler, -i (L). Greens, vegetables
oles, -i (G). Destroy
=oleter (G). A destroyer
olethr, -io, -o, =us (G). Death,
  destruction; deadly
olfact (L). Smell
olid (L). Emitting a smell
olig, -o (G). Few; scant; small
olisth, -em, -mo (G). Slip, slippery
olitor (L). A gardener
oliv, =a, -ace (L). An olive; olive-
  green

=olla (L). A pot or jar
ollym (G). Destroy
olo (G). Whole; destroy
-ology (G). The science of
=olor, -i (L). A swan
olpi, -d, =s (G). A flask
olynth, =us (G). A fig
om, -o (G). The shoulder; raw,
  unripe
-oma (G). A tumor, morbid growth
omal, -o (G). Even
omas, =um (L). A paunch
ombr, -o, =us (G). A rain storm
oment, =um (L). Fat skin
omich, -m (G). Urine
=omma, -t, -to (G). The eye
omni (L). All
omo (G). The shoulder; unripe,
  raw
ompha, -c, =x (g). An unripe grape;
  a young girl
omphal, -i, -o, =us (G). The navel,
  umbilicus; the center; a small
  central projection
onagr, =us (G). A wild ass; a kind
  of plant
onc, -o, =us (G). A mass; a tubercle;
  a hook, barb
oncethm, -o (G). Braying
onch, -o (G). A barb, hook; bulk,
  mass; a tubercle
onci, -o (G). A barb, hook
onco; =oncus (G). A barb, hook; a
  mass; a swelling, tumor
oneir, -o, =us (G). A dream
oner (L). A burden
onir, -o (G). A dream
onisc, =us (G). A wood louse
ono (G). An ass; a beaker
onom, =a, -at, -ato (G). A name
onon, =is (G). A leguminous plant
=onosma (G). An ass smell
onto (G). Being, existing

=onus, -t (L). A burden; burdened
onych, -o (G). A claw, nail
-onym (G). A name
=onyx, -i (G). A claw, nail
oo (G). An egg
oodeo (G). Egg-shaped
oophor (G). An ovary
op (L). Reversed, against
op, =s (G). The face, appearance; the voice
opac (L). Shaded, dull
opal, -in, -o, =us (G). An opal
ope, -o (G). An opening
opera (L). Work
opercul, =um (L). A cover, lid
ophel, -o, =us (G). Use, service
ophi, -d, -o, =s (G). A snake, serpent
ophiur (G). Serpent-tailed
ophry, -o, =s (G). The eyebrow, brow
ophthalm, -i, -o, =us (G). The eye
opi, -a, -o, =um (G). Poppy juice, opium
-opia (G). Vision
opiso (G). Backward
opisth, -i, -o (G). Behind, the hind part
opl, -o (G). Armor; a tool
oplit, =es (G). Heavily armed; an armed soldier
opo (G). The face; juice
opor (G). Autumn
opoter, -o (G). Either
oppil (L). Stop up, block
opposit (L). Opposite
=ops (G). Appearance; the face; the voice
opsi, -o (G). Appearance; sight; late
opso (G). Meat, dainty food

opt, -i, -o (G). The eye; vision
opt, -a, -i (L). Choose
opter (G). An observer, scout
optes (G). Roast
opti (L): Choose; (G): the eye; vision
optim (L). Best
opto (G). The eye; vision; roasted
opul (L). Rich
ora (L). Mouth
=orama (G). A view
orari (L). Coastal; a napkin
oras, -i (G). Sight
orbi, -t, -to (L). A circle, track, orbit
orc, =a (L). A whale
orches, -t (G). Dancing
orchi, -d, -do, =s (G). The testicle; a plant named from the shape of its roots
orcho (G). A testicle
orcul, =a, -i (L). A cask
ore, -o (G). A mountain
=oreades (G). Mountain nymphs
orect, -o (G). Stretched out
oreg (G). Desire
oress, -i (G). Mountains
orex, -i (G). Desire, appetite
organ, -o (G). An organ, instrument
orgi (G). Secret rites
orgyi, =a (G). The length of the outstretched arms
ori (L): The mouth; (G): a mountain
oribat (G). Mountain-roaming
orient, -al (L). Rising; east
origin (L). Arise, begin
orism, =a (G). A limitation, boundary
orm, -o (G). A cord, chain
ornat (L). Adorned
orneo (G). A bird; a plume
orni, =s, -th, -tho (G). A bird

oro (G): A mountain; (L): the
  mouth
oront, =es (G). A river in Syria
oroph, =a, -o (G). A roof
orphan (G). Without parents;
  bereft
orphe (My). Melodious
orphn, -o (G). Dark, dusky
orrh, -o, =us (G). Serum; the
  end of the sacrum
ortali, -d, =s (G). A fowl; a young
  bird
orth, -o (G). Straight, upright
orthagorisc, =us (G). A suckling
  pig
orthrio (G). Early, at daybreak
orty, -g, =x (G). A quail
oruss (G). Dig through, burrow
orych, -o (G). Dig
oryct, -er, -o (G). Dug out; a
  digger; a fossil
oryg (G). An antelope; a digging
  tool
oryss (G). Dig through, burrow
=oryx (G). An antelope; a digging
  tool
oryz, =a, -i, -o (G). Rice
=os (L). A bone; a mouth
-os, =a, =um, =us (L). Full of
osche, -o (G). The scrotum
oscho (G). A young branch
oscill, -a, -o (L). Swing back and
  forth
oscin, -i (L). A singing bird
oscit (L). Yawning, drowsiness
oscul (L). Kiss; a little mouth
-ose (L). Full of
-osis (L). A condition of
-osis (G). A disease
-osity (L). Fullness
 osm, =a, -i, -o (G). A smell,
  odor

osmo, -s, -t (G). Pushing, thrusting
osmund, =a (NL). A kind of fern
osphr, -a, -e, -o (G). A smell,
  scent
osphy, -o, =s (G). The loin, hip
oss, -e, -i (L). A bone
ossic (L). A little bone
ost, -e, -eo, =eum (G). A bone
oster, -o (G). Nimble
osti, =um (L). A small opening,
  door
ostr, -e, =ea, -i, -in (L). An
  oyster; purple
ostrac, -o, =um (G). A shell;
  earthenware
ostry, =a (G). A hardwood tree
-osu, =m, =s (L). Full of
ot, -i, -o (G). The ear
othe, -o (G). Push, thrust
othni, -o (G). Strange, foreign
otid, -o (G). An ear; a bustard
otio, -n (G). A kind of shellfish
otios (L). Idle, at leisure
=otis (G). A bustard
oto; =otus (G). An ear
ouden (G). None
oulo (G). Woolly, with thick hair;
  the gums; a scar; whole
our, =a (G). The tail
ouran, -i, -o (G). Heaven
ouro (G). Urine; a guard; a wild
  bull
-ous (E). Full of
ov, -i, =um (L). An egg
ovari, -o, =um (L). An ovary
ovat (L). Egg-shaped
ovi (L). An egg; a sheep
ovin (L). Of sheep
ovipar (L). Egg-laying
=ovis (L). A sheep
ovul, =um (L). A little egg

=ovum (L). An egg
ox, -a, -i, -y, =ys (G). Sharp, acute; acid
oxal, =is (G). Sorrel
oxe, -o (G). Sharp; vinegar
oxid (G): Sharp; (F): containing oxygen
oxy, =s (G). Sharp; acid
=oxyechus (G). A sharp sound
oxysm (G). Sharpen
oz, -o (G). Smell; a branch
ozot, -o (G). Branched

P

pabul, =um (L). Food; fodder
pach, -y (G). Thick
pachn, =a, -o (G). White frost
paci (L). Peace
pact (L). Made fast, solid
paed, -a, -o (G). A child
=paedia (G). Education
paedid (L). Stinking
=paegma, -to (G). Sport
pag, -o, =us (G). A rock; ice, frost
pagan, =us (L). A rustic, peasant
pagi, -o (G). Fixed, fastened, firm
pagin, =a (L). A leaf or page
pago; =pagus (G). A rock; ice, frost
pagur, -o, =us (G). A crab
paid, -o (G). A child
pal, =a (L). A shovel, spade
pal, -ae, -aeo (G). Ancient
pal, -i, =us (L). A stake
palam, =a (G). The palm of the hand
palamed, =es (G My). Cunning, art
palass, -o (G). Spot, defile
palat, -i, -o, =um (L). The roof of the mouth, palate
pale (G). Wrestle, fight

pale, =a, -i (L). Chaff, straw
pale, -o (G). Ancient
palest (G). Wrestling, fighting
palett, =a (L). A little spade
pali (L). A stake
pali, -n (G). Again, back
palinur, =us (My). The pilot of Aeneas
pall, -ens, -esc, -id, -or (L). Pale
palla, -c, =x (G). A concubine; a youth
palli, -at, -o, =um (L). A mantle; cloaked
pallo (G). Sway, quiver
palm, =a, -i (L). A palm tree; the palm of the hand
palm, -o (G). Vibrating, throbbing
palmat, -i (L). Webbed, palmate
palp (L). Touch, feel
=palpator (L). A feeler
palpebr, =a (L). An eyelid; wink, blink
palpi (L). A feeler, palp
palpit (L). Throb
palt, -o, =um (G). A dart
palu, -di, -str (L). A marsh, swamp
=palus (L). A stake; a marsh, swamp
pam, -m (G). All
pampin, =us (L). A tendril
pan (G). All; a torch
pan, -i, =is (L). Bread
panace (G). All-healing
pand (L). Spread out; bend
panic, =um (L). Panic grass
pandion (G My). A king of Athens
pani, =s (L). Bread
panicul, =a (L). A tuft
=panicum (L). Panic grass
pann, =us (L). Cloth, rags
pannicul (L). A thin sheet, a rag
pano (G). A torch
pans (L). Expanded

pant, -a, -e, -i, -o (G). All
panurg (G). Ready to do anything
pany (G). Altogether, exceedingly
=papaver, -i (L). The poppy
=papilio, -n (L). A butterfly
papill, =a, -i (L). A nipple
papp, -o, =us (G). A grandfather;
   down, fuzz
papul, =a (L). A pimple
papyr, -i, =us (L). Paper, papyrus
par (L). Bear, give birth to
par, -a (G). Beside, beyond, near
par, -i (L). Equal; a titmouse
paradis (G). A park, pleasure
   ground
paradox, -o (G). Incredible,
   marvelous
parallel, -i, -o (G). Parallel
paramec (G). Oblong, oval
paraphron (G). Mad, insane, dis-
   traught
parapod (G). At the feet of,
   close by
parasit, -i, -o (G). Near food; eat
   at another's table; a parasite
parat (L). Ready, prepared
parci (L). Few, sparing
pard, -o, =us (G). A leopard
pardal (G). Spotted; a starling
parei, =a (G). The cheek
paren, -t (L). A parent
paresi, =s (G). A letting go; paraly-
   sis, impairment of strength
pari (L). Equal; a titmouse
pari, =a (G). The cheek
parie, =s, -t (L). A wall
=parilla (L). A little vine
parm, =a (L). A small shield
parod, -o, =us (G). An entrance,
   passage
paronym (G). Of the same derivation

parot, -i (G). Beside the ear
parotid, -o (G). The parotid gland
-parous (L). Giving birth to, bearing
=pars (L). A part
parsi (L). Few, sparing
parthen, -o (G). A virgin; without
   fertilization
parti (L). A part
partim (L). Partly
partit (L). Divided
partur, -i (L). Bring forth young,
   give birth to
parul (L). A little titmouse
=parus (L). A titmouse
parv, -i (L). Small
paryph, =a, -o (G). A border
pas, -i (G). All
pasc, -u, =uus (L). Feed; a pasture
paspal (G). A kind of millet; fine
   meal
=passer, -i (L). A sparrow
passi (L). Passion; suffer; pace;
   spread out
passul, =a (L). A small raisin
past (G): Sprinkle; (L): food
pastill, =us (L). A small loaf
pasteur, -i (N). Louis Pasteur
pastin (L). Dig; a parsnip
=pastio, -n (L). Keeping, feeding
=pastor, -i (L). A shepherd, keeper
pat, -i (G). A path, walk
pataec (My). A dwarfish deity of
   Phoenicia
patag, -o, =us (G). A clatter
patagi, =um (L). A border
patell, =a, -i, -o (L). A little dish
paten, -t (L). Spreading, open
=pater (L). A father; a flat dish
patern (L). Of a father
patet (G). Walk
path, -o, =y (G). Suffering, disease
pati (G). A walk, path

patibul, =um (L). A yoke for criminals

patien, -t (L). Suffering

patin, =a (L). A bowl

patr, -i, -o (L). A father

patri, -a, -o (G). Fatherland; habitat

patul (L). Open, spreading

=patus (G). A walk, path

pauc, -i (L). Few

paul, -i, -o (L). Little, small

paur, -o (G). Little, small

paus (G). Cessation

pav, -e, -i, -o (L). Quake, tremble

pavid (L). Trembling, timid

=pavo, -n (L). A peacock

=pax (L). Peace

paxill, =us (L). A peg

pec, -o (G). Comb

pecc (L). Sin, transgress

pechy, =s (G). The forearm

pecor, -i (L). A herd

pect, =en, -in, -o (L). A comb

pect, -o (G). Fixed, congealed

pect, -or, =us (L). The breast

pecu, -d, =s (L). Cattle

peculiar (L). One's own

ped, -a, -e, -i, -o (L): A foot; (G): a child; the earth; a fetter; an oar

pedal (L). Of a foot

pedali, =um (G). A rudder; a kind of plant

pedan, -o (G). Short

pedat, -i (L). Having feet

pede, -m, -si, -t (G). Leap, leaping

pedetent (G). Step by step

pedetic (G). Leaping

pedi (G): A child; (L): a foot

pedi, -o (G). Plains; the instep; a fetter

=pedia (G). Education; a child

=pediaecetes (G). A plains dweller

pedic, -l, -ul (L). A little foot

pedicul, -ari, -os, =us (L). A louse

pedil, -o, =us (G). A sandal

pedin, -o (G). Found on the plains

pedio (G). Plains; the instep; a fetter

pedo (G): A child; the earth; an oar; (L): a foot

peduncul, =us (NL). A little foot

peg, -o (G). A fountain; solid

pegas, =us (G My). A winged horse

=pegma, -t (G). Congealed, fixed; a framework

pein, =a, -o (G). Hunger

peir, =a (G). A trial

peith, -i (G). Persuade

pejor (L). Bad; deterioration

pel, -o (G). Clay, mud; brown, dusky

pelad (F). Bald

pelag, -i, -o, =us (G). The sea

pelarg, -o, =us (G). A stork

pelec, -an, =anus, -in (G). A pelican

pelec, -y (G). A hatchet, axe

peli, -o (G). Livid, black and blue

=pelia (G). A dove

pelichn, =a (G). A bowl

pelico (G). A basin; the pelvis

pelidn, -o (G). Livid, black and blue

pelio (G). Livid, black and blue

pell, =a, -i (G). Skin; the pelvis; a bowl, basin

pell, -o (G). Dusky

pellen (L). Driving

pelluc, -en, -id (L). Transparent

=pelma, -to (G). The sole of the foot; a stalk

pelo (G). Clay, mud; brown, dusky

pelor, -o (G). A monster; monstrous

=pelorus (My). Hannibal's pilot

pelt, =a (G). A shield

pelv, -eo, -i, -io (L). A basin; the pelvis

pely, -co, =x (G). A basin; the
  pelvis
pempheri, =s (G). A kind of fish
pemphi, -g, =x (G). A blister,
  pimple
=pemphredon (G). A kind of wasp
pen, -e (L). Almost, nearly
pench (F). Incline
pend, -an, -en, -ul (L). Hang,
  hanging
pene, -s, -st, -t (G). A laborer
penelope (My). The wife of
  Ulysses
penetr (L). Enter, pierce
peni, =s (L). The penis
penichr, -o (G). Poor, needy
penicill, =um (L). A pencil,
  brush
penit (L). Inner, from the inside
penn, =a, -ati, -i (L). A feather;
  a wing; feathered
pens, -a (L). Weigh
pensil (L). Hang, hanging
pent, -a (G). Five
pentecost (G). The fiftieth
penteteri (G). Every five years
penth, -est, -o (G). Sorrow; a
  mourner
penult (L). Next to the last
penuri (L). Want; in want
peo, =s (G). The penis
pep, -s, -t (G). Digest; cook
pepast (G). Ripen
peper, -i, -o (G). Pepper
pepino (Sp). Cucumber
pepita (Sp). A gold nugget; a
  melon seed
pepl, -a, -o, =um (G). A gown,
  coat
pepo, -n (G). Ripe; a melon
peps, -i (G). Digest; cook
pept, -i, -o (G). Digested; cooked

per (L). Through, by means of
per, =a, -o (G). A pouch
per, -o (G). Maimed, mutilated
perc, =a, -i (G). The perch
percn, -o (G). Dusky
percol, -a (L). Filter through
perd (L). Lose
perd, -ic, =ix (G). A partridge
perdit (L). Lost, destroyed
peregrin (L). Wander, travel
  abroad
pereio (G). On the other side
perenni (L). Through the year
perfora (L). Bore through
perfunct (L). Performed
pergamen, =a (L). Parchment
peri (G). Around
perideri, =s (G). A necklace
peridi, =um (G). A little pouch
peridin (G). Whirled about
perine (G). Near the anus
perio (G). On the other side
peripat, -etic (G). Walking about
peripher, =ia (G). The circum-
  ference, outer surface or border
periphor, =a (G). A circuit
periss, -o (G). Superfluous; odd
  in number
perister, =a (G). A dove, pigeon
peristole (G). A contraction
peritone, =um (L). The membrane
  around the intestines
perjur (L). Lying, false
perl, =a (NL). A kind of insect
perman, -en (L). Remain, remaining
permea (L). Pass through
pern, =a (G). A shellfish; a ham
perni, =s (NL). The honey-buzzard
pernic, -i (L). Destructive; quick,
  agile
pero (G). Maimed; a pouch

=pero, -n (L). A rawhide boot
peron, -e, -eo, -i, -o (G). A
  brooch; the fibula
=persea (G). A sacred tree in
  Egypt and Persia
persic, =a (L). A peach
=persona, -t (L). A mask; masked
perspic, -at, -i (L). See through;
  sharp-sighted
perspicillat (L). Conspicuous
perth, -a, -o (G). Get by plunder
=perula (G). A little pouch, wallet
-pes (L). A foot
pess, -o (G). An oval pebble; a
  checkerboard
pessim (L). The worst
pessul, =us (L). A bolt
pesti, =s (L). A pest, plague
pet, -it (L). Seek
peta, -ci, =x (L). Greedy
petal, -o, =um (G). A leaf; spread
  out, flat
petas, -m, =ma (G). Anything
  spread out, a curtain
petaur, -o, =um (G). A perch,
  springboard
petechi (L). With red spots on
  the skin
petig, -in, -o (L). A scab
petil (L). Slender, thin
petin, -o (G). Winged, flying
petiol, -a, =us (L). A stalk,
  petiole
petit (L). Seek
petr, =a, -o (G). A rock, stone
petun (F). Tobacco
peuc, =a, -e, -o (G). Pine, fir
peucedan, =um (G). Hog fennel
pex, -i, =is, -y (G). A fixation,
  fastening
pexi (L). Woolly
pez, =a, -i, -o (G). The foot,
  bottom; on foot

phabo (G). A dove, pigeon
phac, -a, -o, =us (G). A lentil;
  a lens; the lens of the eye
phacel, -o, =us (G). A bundle,
  cluster
phae, -o (G). Dusky
phaedr, -o (G). Bright, radiant
phaen, -o (G). Show
phaetho, -nt (G). Shining
phag, =e, -o (G). Eat
phak, -o (G). A lentil; a lens
phal, -o (G). Shining, white
phalacr, -o (G). Bald
phalaen, =a (G). A moth; a whale
phalan, -g, -ge, -go, =x (g). A
  bone of the finger or toe; a battle
  line
phalar, -i, =is, -o (G). A coot
phalar, -o (G). White-crested
phaler, -a, -o (L): A metallic ornament; (G): white-crested
phall, -o, =us (G). The penis
phan (G). Show, appear
phane, -r, -ro (G). Visible
phantas, -mo (G). Fantasy, fancy;
  showing
phanto (G). Visible
phao, =s (G). Light
=phaps (G). A dove, pigeon
phar, -o (G). A piece of cloth; a
  lighthouse; a plow
pharan, -g, =x (G). A cleft, gulley
pharci, -d, =s (G). A wrinkle
pharm, -ac, -aceu, -aco (G). A
  drug; a poison
pharo (G). A lighthouse; a piece of
  cloth; a plow
pharyn, -g, -ge, -go, =x (G). The
  throat, pharynx
phas, =ia, =is, =y (G). Speech
phasc, =um (G). A tree moss
phascol, -o (G). A leather bag
phase (G). Appearance, show; shine

phaseol (G). A kidney bean
phasgan, -o, =um (G). A sword
phasia (G). Speech
phasian, =us (G). A pheasant
-phasis (G). Speech
phasm, a, -ato, -i (G). An ap-
  parition, phantom
phassa (G). The ring dove
-phasy (G). Speech
phatn, -i, -o (G). A tooth socket
phausi (G). Shining bright
pheg, -o, =us (G). An oak
pheid, -o, -ol (G). Thrifty
phell, -o (G). Cork
phelli, -o (G). Stony ground
phem, =y (G). Speak, report
phena, -c, =x (G). Purple-red;
  a cheat
phenacist, -o (G). Deceitful
phene (G). A kind of vulture
pheng, -o (G). Light
pheni, -c, -g (G). Deep red
pheno (G). Show, seem, appear;
  purple-red
pheny (G). Deep red
pheo (G). Dusky, gray
pher (G). Carry, bear
pherb (G). To feed
phet (G). Speak
pheug, -o (G). Flee
phial, =a (G). A saucer
phiar, -o (G). Bright, shining;
  sleek
phibal, -i, -o (G). A kind of
  fig; a kind of myrtle
phil, -a, -i, -o (G). Love, loving
philatel (F). A stamp collection
philedon, -o (G). Fond of pleasure
phillyr (G). A shrub
philo (G). Love, loving
philomel (G). A nightengale
philydr, -o (G). Water-loving

philypn, -o (G). Sleep-loving
philyr, =a (G). The linden tree
phimo (G). Muzzle, shut up
phlao (G). Eat greedily
phlasm (G). Bruise
phlaur, -o (G). Trivial, useless
phleb, -o (G). A vein
phleg, -eth, -ethon, -o (G). Burn
phlegm, =a, -asi, -ato (G). Inflammation, mucus
phleo (G). A marsh reed
=phleps (G). A vein
=phleum (G). A water plant, a
  rush
phlib, -o (G). Squeeze
phlips, -i (G). Squeeze
phloe, -o (G). The bark of a tree
phlog, -i, -mo, -o (G). A flame,
  burning
phlogist, -o (G). Burnt
phlogo, =sis (G). Flame; inflammation
phlor, -o (G). The bark of a tree
=phlox (G). A flame
phlycten, =a, -o (G). A blister
phlysi, =s (G). An eruption
phlyz (G). Inflame; a blister
phlyzaci (G). A small blister
phob, =ia, -o (G). Fear, dread
phober, -o (G). Formidable, fearful
phobetic, -o (G). Timid
phobetr, -o (G). A soothsayer
=phobia; phobo (G). Fear, dread
phoc, =a, -i (G). A seal
phocaen, =a (G). A porpoise
phoeb, -o (G). Shine; bright
phoebe (from its call). The phoebe
phoeni, -c, -co, =x (G). Purple, reddish purple; the date palm
phola, -d, =s (G). Lurking in a hole;
  a mollusc
pholc, -o (G). Squint-eyed; bandy-
  legged

phole, -o (G). A lurking place,
  den
pholi, -do, =s (G). A scale;
  scaly
phon (G). Sound, voice; kill
phon, =a, -e, -et, -i, -o (G).
  Sound, voice
phont, =es (G). A murderer
phor (G). A thief; a kind of bee
phor, -a, -e, -i, -o (G). Carry,
  bear; movement
phorb, =a (G). Feed, pasture,
  fodder
phorbei, =a (G). A halter
phorc, -o (G). Gray
phore; phori (G). Carry, bear
phorm, -i, -o (G). Wickerwork;
  a mat; a basket
phoro (G). Bear, carry; movement
phortic, -o (G). Vulgar, common
=phos; phot, -a, -i, -o (G). Light
phox, -o (G). Pointed
phoyx (G). A kind of heron
phrac, -t (G). Fence in
phragm, =a, -it, -o (G). A fence,
  partition
phras, -a, -e, -eo, -i (G). Speech
phraster (G). A guide
phrater, -o (G). Brothers
phrax, -i (G). An obstruction
phreat, -i (G). A well, tank
phren, -i, -ico, -o (G). A dia-
  phragm; the heart, mind
phreoryct, =es, -i (G). A well
  digger
phric, -o (G). Shiver, shudder,
  bristle up
phris, -o, -so (G). Ruffle up
=phrix, -o (G). Bristling
phron, -ema (G). The mind,
  spirit

phronim, -i, -o (G). Understanding, wise, discrete
phrur, -o (G). A guard
phryct (G). A burning torch; a kind
  of gum
phryg (G). Dry; roast
phrygan, -o (G). A dry stick
phryn, =a, -o (G). A toad
phthalm, -o (G). The eye
phthan (G). Arrive first
phthar, -s, -to (G). Corruptible,
  mortal, transitory
phtheir (G). Destroy, waste; lice;
  a kind of pine cone
phthi, -no, -si, -so (G). Waste away;
  consumption
phthir (G). Lice
phthon, -o (G). Malice
phthong (G). A sound, voice
phthor, =a (G). Destruction, de-
  composition
phy, -a, -o (G). Grow, produce
phyc, -o, =us (G). Seaweed; painted
phye (G). Growth, stature
phyg, -o (G). Shun, flee
phyl, -et, -o, =um (G). A tribe
phyla, -ct, -cto, -xi (G). Watch,
  guard, preserve
phyll, -o, =um (G). A leaf
=phyma, -t, -to (G). A tumor, swelling
phymos (G). Swollen
phyo (G). Grow, produce
phys, -a, -i (G). Blow; nature; a
  bladder
physal, -i, =is (G). A bladder,
  bubble; a wind instrument
physal, -o, =us (G). A toad; a kind
  of whale
physc, =a, -o, -on (G). The large
  intestine; a sausage; a blister
physem (G). Breathe; snorting, raging;
  inflate, blow

physi (G). Blow; nature; a bladder

physic, -o (G). Physical, natural

physio (G). Nature

physo (G). Bellows; a bladder, air sac, bubble

phyt, -o, =um (G). A plant

phyzel, -o (G). Shy

pi (L). Pious; tender

piacul (L). Atone, expiate

piar, -o (G). Fat, tallow

pic, =a (L). A magpie

pic, -i (L). A woodpecker; variegated

picar (L). Of pitch

pice (L). Pitch black

pice, =a (L). Pitch pine, spruce

pici (L). A woodpecker; variegated, speckled

picin (L). Pitch black

pico (L). Smear with pitch

picr, -i, -o (G). Bitter, pungent

pict (L). Painted, variegated

pida, -c, =x (G). A fountain or spring

=pieris (G My). One of the Muses

pies, -m, -t (G). Squeeze

piezo (G). Squeeze

pigment, =um (L). Paint

pign, -er, =us (L). A pledge

pigo (G). The rump

pigr (L). Slow, sluggish

pil, =a (L). A ball; a mortar

pil, -i, =us (L). Hair

pile, -i, -o, =us (L). A cap

pileat (L). Capped

pilidi, -o, =um (G). A small felt cap

pilo (G). A cap; felt

pilos (L). Hairy

=pilus (L). Hair

pimel, -e, -o (G). Fat, lard

pin, -i, =us (L). Pine

pin, -o (G). Drink; dirt, filth; hungry

pina, -c, =x (G). A board, plank

pinar, -o (G). Dirty

pine (L). Shaped like a pine cone

pinet (L). Pine wood

pingu, -i, -o (L). Fat, stout

pini (L). Pine

pinn, =a (G). A kind of mussel

pinn, =a, -i (L). A feather; a wing

pinnat (L). Feathered, pinnate

pino (G). Drink; dirt, filth; hungry

=pinus (L). Pine

pio, -n (L). Fat, rich

pipatio, -n (L). Chirping

=piper, -at, -i (L). Pepper; peppery

pipi, -en (L). Peeping, chirping

pipil, -o (L). Chirp, peep

pipistrell (It). A bat

pipr (G). A woodpecker

pipt, -o (G). Fall

pir, -i, =um (L). A pear

pirang, =a (Br). A tanager

pirat, =a, -ic (L). A pirate; piratical

pis, -i, -o, =us (G). A pea; meadows

pisc, -i, =is (L). A fish

piscin, =a (L). A fish pond

piscinari, =us (L). One fond of fish ponds

piss, =a (G). Pitch

pissod (G). Pitch-like

pist, -i, -o (G). Liquid; genuine, trusted

pistaci (G). A kind of tree

pistill, -i, =um (L). A pestle

=pisus (G). A pea; meadows

pitang, =us (Br). A flycatcher

pith, -o, =us (G). A wine jar

pithan, -o (G). Plausible

pithec, -o, =us (G). An ape

pitt, =a (G): Pitch; (NL): a kind of bird

pituit, -ar (L). A secretion of mucus

pity, -o, =s (G). Pine, fir

pityr, -o, =um (G). Bran, refuse

=pix (L). Pitch

plac, -o (G). A tablet, plate; flat

placat (L). Please, appease

placent, =a, -i (L). A round flat cake; the placenta

placid (L). Smooth, pleasing

placin, -o (G). Made of boards

placo (G). A tablet, plate; flat

pladar, -o (G). Wet, damp

plag, =a (L). A blow, stripe; a region, zone; a snare

plagat (L). Streaked, striped

plagi, -o (G). Oblique, sideways; the sides

plagia, -r, -t (L). A kidnapper

plan, -i (L). Flat, level

plan, -o (G). Wandering

plane, -s, -t, =tes (G). A wanderer, rover

plankt, -o (G). Wandering

plant, =a, -i (L). The sole of the foot; a plant

plantag, -in, =o (L). Plantain

plas, -i, -o (G). Form, mold, shape

plasm, =a, -ato, -o (G). Something molded or modeled; plasm

plasso (G). Form, mold, shape

plast, -o (G). Formed, molded; counterfeit

plastr, -on (F). A breastplate

-plasty (G). Growth, molding

plat, -e, -i, -y (G). Broad, flat

plata, -c, =x (G). A kind of fish

platale, =a (L). The spoonbill

platan, =us (G). The sycamore

plate (G). Broad, flat

platess, -a, -i (L). The plaice

plati; platy (G). Broad, flat

plaus (L). Applaud

plaut (L). Flat-footed

plebe, -i (L). Of common people; common

plec, -o, -t, -to (G). Twine, twist, braid; strike; twisted

plect, -r, -ro, =rum (G). A strike; a spur

pleg, -a, -e, -i, =ia, -o (G). A blow, strike; a sickle

plegm, =a, -ato, -o (G). Wickerwork

plei, -o (G). More; full

pleist, -o (G). Most

plen, -i (L). Full

pleo (G). Full; more; sail, swim

pleon (G). More, full

pler, -o, -om, -os (G). Full, fullness, filling

plesi, -o (G). Near, recent

pletho, -r (G). Full, fullness; in excess

plethy, -sm, -smo (G). Fullness; increase, enlargement

pleur, -a, -i, -o, =um (G). The side; a rib

pleuroth, -en, -o (G). From the side

pleust (G). A sailor; sailing

plex, -i, =us (L). Interwoven; a network

plexi, -o, =s (G). A stroke, percussion

plic, -o (L). Fold, braid

plinth, -o, =us (G). A brick

plio (G). More

ploc, -io, -o, =us (G). Weave, braid, twist; a curl of hair

plocam, -o (G). A lock of hair

plocar (G). Something woven

ploce, -i, =us (G). A weaver, braider

plocio, ploco; =plocus (G). A braid, a curl of hair; weave, twist

ploiari, =um (G). A small boat

ploim (G). Sailing, fit for sailing

plor, -an (L). Wail, wailing

plot, -er, -i, -o (G). Floating, drifting; sailing; swimming

plum, =a, -e, -i (L). A feather
plumb, -e, =eus (L). Lead
plumbag, -in, =o (L). Leadwort
plur, -i (L). More, several
=plus (L). More, in addition
plusi, -a, -o (G). Rich, wealthy
plut, -o (G). Riches, wealth
plute, =us (L). A shed, parapet
plutoni (NL). Dusky
pluvi, =us (L). Rain
plynteri, -o (G). Washing
plysi, =s (G). A washing
pne, -o, -u, -um, -us (G).
   Breath; breathe
=pneuma, -ti, -to (G). Wind, air,
   breath
pneumo, -n, -no (G). The lungs
pneus, -i, =is, -o (G). Blowing,
   breathing
pnig, -o (G). Choke, suffocate
pno, -i (G). Air; breathing
=pnyx (G N). A crowd
po, =a, -e, -o (G). Grass, a
   grassy place
poc, -o, =us (G). Fleece
poca, -do, =s (G). Hair, wool
pocill, =um (L). A little cup
pocul, =um (L). A cup; a draught
pod, -o, =y (G). A foot
podabr, -o (G). Tender-footed
podarg, -o (G). Swift-footed
=podex (L). The rump; the anus
podi, =um (G). A foot
podic, -i (L). The rump; the anus
podo; =pody (G). A foot
poe (G). Grass, a grassy place
poecil, -i, -o (G). Variegated,
   many-colored; varied
pogo, =n, -ni, -no (G). A beard
poie, =sis, -t (G). Make, produce
poikil, -o (G). Varied; variegated
=poimen, -o (G). A shepherd; a
   herd

pol, -i (G). Sell; an axis
polar, -i (L). Of the pole, polarity
polem, -i, -o (G). War; hostile
poli (G). Sell; a city
poli, -a, -o (G). Gray
-polis (G). A city; a citizen
polist, =es (G). The founder of a
   city
polit (G): A citizen; (L): polished,
   refined
poll (L). Be strong
poll, =en, -in (L). Fine flour
poll, =ex, -ic (L). The thumb; the
   big toe
pollac, -i (G). Many, often
pollut (L). Defiled
polo (G). An axis; a young animal
poly (G). Many, much
polybor, -o (G). Greedy
polyp, -i, -o (G). Many-footed; a
   polyp
polyphem, =us (G My). A one-eyed
   giant
polypodi (G). Many-footed; a kind
   of fern
pom, -o, =um (L). An apple, fruit
poma, -to (G). A lid, cover; a
   drink
pomp, =a (G). A guide
pomph, -o, =us (G). A blister
pompholy, -g, -go, =x (G). A bubble
pompil, =us (L). A kind of fish
=pomum (L). An apple, fruit
pon, -o, =us (G). Toil; pain
=pons (L). A bridge
ponder (L). Weighty
poner, -i, -o (G). Pain; bad, painful
pono (G). Toil; pain
pont, -i (L). A bridge
pont, -o (G). The sea
=ponus (G). Toil; pain
poo (G). Grass, a grassy place

=pooecetes (G). A grass dweller
popl, =es, -it (L). The back of
  the knee
popul, =us (L). People; the poplar
por, -i, =us (L). A pore, small
  opening
por, -o (G). A soft stone; blind;
  a callus
porc, -i, =us (L). A hog, swine
porcat (NL). Ridged
porcell, -i, =us (L). A little
  pig; a sowbug
porcellan (It). Porcelain
porci (L). A hog, swine
porcin (L). Of a hog; pork
=porcus (L). A hog, swine
pore, -i; -ut (G). A passage;
  convey, traverse
pori (L). A pore, small opening
porist, -o (G). Provided
porn, -o (G). A prostitute
poro (G). A hardening, callus; a
  soft stone; blind
porp, =a (G). A buckle, brooch
porpa, -c, =x (G). A ring, loop;
  a handle
porphy--, -io, -o (G). Purple
porr, -i, =um, =s (L). A leek
porrect (L). Stretched out, ex-
  tended forward
port (L). Carry
port, =a, -i (L). A gate, door
port, -i, -un, =us (L). A harbor,
  port
porth, -e, -o (G). Destroy
porthmi, -d, =s (G). A narrow
  passage
porti (L). A gate, door; a harbor,
  port
portulac, =a (L). Purslane
portun (L My). A harbor, port
porulos (L). Full of small pores

=porus (L). A pore, small opening
porzan, =a (It). A rail
pos, =is (G). Drink; a husband
pos, -o (G). How much; indefinitely;
  quantity
poseidon (G My). A god of the sea
posit (L). Placed
post (L). Behind, after
post, -er, -ero, -ic (L). Hinder,
  posterior
posth, -i, -o (G). The foreskin; the
  penis
postul (L). Demand
pot, -a, -i, -o (G). Drink
potam, -o, =us (G). A river
potass, -i (NL). Potash, potassium
poten, -t (L). Powerful
poter, -i, -io, =ium (G). A drinking
  cup
potero (G). Either
potes (G). A drinker
poth, -o, =us (G): Longing, desire;
  (NL): a kind of plant
poti, poto (G). Drink
=pous (G). A foot
pra, -o (G). Mild, gentle
pract (L). Do, act, work
prae (L). Before
praeco, -c, =x (L). Early, premature
praesep (L). An enclosure
praeter (L). Beyond, past, more than
praeust (L). Scorched
praevar (L). Irregular
=pragma, -to (G). An object, thing,
  fact, matter
pragmon (G). Work
praniz (G). Thrown headlong
prao (G). Mild, gentle
pras, -eo, -in, =um (G). A leek
prat, -i, =um (L). A meadow
pratens (L). Found in meadows
prav (L). Deformed

prax, =is (G). An exercise,
  action
pre (L). Before
preca (L). Pray, request
preco, -ci, =x (L). Early, premature
preda (L). Prey, booty
predi, =um (L). A farm, estate
pregnan, -t (L). With child,
  pregnant
premn, -o, =um (G). A tree trunk,
  stem
pren, =es, -o (G). Drooping, bent
  forward
preniz (G). Thrown headlong
prep, -o (G). Visible, conspicuous; resemble
prept, -o (G). Distinguished
presby, =s, -t (G). Old; an old
  person
preter (L). Beyond, past, more
  than
priap, =us (G My). The god of
  procreation; the penis
prim, -a, -i (L). First
primul, =us (L). The primrose
prin, -o, =us (G). A kind of oak
princip, -ali (L). First place,
  chief; principal
=prion, -o (G). A saw
pris (G). Sawing; a saw
prisc (L). Primitive, ancient
prisma, -t, -to (G). Something
  sawed; a prism
prist, -i, -io, -o (G). Sawed
pristin (L). Primitive; old-
  fashioned
priv, -a, -i (L). An individual, one
  each
pro (G). Before, in front of, forward; instead of, for
prob (L). Test, examine; good

proble, -s, -t (G). Projecting
probol, -o, =us (G). A weapon, bul-
  wark
probosc, -i (G). That which exam-
  ines; a proboscis
procell, =a (L). A storm
procer (L). Tall, high
process (L). Project from; advance
prochyn (G). Kneeling
proct, -o, =us (G). The anus; the
  rectum
procumben (L). Prostrate
prod, -i (L). Disclose, reveal
prodig (L). Wasteful, lavish
prodigios (L). Marvel, marvelous
prodot, -o (G). Betrayed
prodrom, =us (L). A kind of fig
proeo (G). Early
profund (L). Deep
progn, =e (L My). A swallow
proi, -o (G). Early
prol, -i (L). Offspring
prolep, =sis, -t (G). Anticipation
promach, -o, =us (G). A challenger
prometh, =ea (G). Foresight
prominen, -t (L). Projecting
pron (L): Bent forward; (G): a
  promontory
propaga (L). Generate
propinqu (L). Near
propior, -i (L). Nearer
propri (L). One's own, peculiar
pror, =a (G). The prow of a ship
prors (L). Forward; absolutely
pros, -o (G). To; before
prosop, -o, =um (G). The counte-
  nance, face
prosopi, =s (G). A kind of plant
prosphor, -o (G). Convenient,
  fitting
prostat, -o (ML). The prostate
  gland

prosth, -en, -o (G). Before; forward

prosthe, -c, -m (G). An appendage, addition

prot, -e, -o (G). First, original

protero (G). Fore, former

=proteus (G My). A god that could
assume various forms

protist, -o (G). The very first

proto (G). First, original

provid (L). Cautious

proxim (L). Nearest

pruin, =a, -o (L). Hoar frost

prun, =us (L). The plum

=prunella (Ger). A throat disease

pruri, -t (L). Itch

prymn, -o, =us (G). The hindmost; the stern of a ship

psaca, -d, =s (G). A small
broken-off piece

psaer, -o (G). Flutter, touch
lightly

psal, -i, -id,,-o (G). Scissors

psalist, -o (G). Clipped

psallo (G). Twang, pluck

psalm, =a, -i, -o (G). A tune
played on a stringed instrument;
a psalm; a twitching

psalo (G). Scissors

psalter (G). A harp player; a book
of many leaves

psamm, -o, =us (G). Sand

psar, -o (G). Speckled; the starling

psathy, -o (G). Crumbling

psectr, =a, -o (G). A scraper

psedn, -o (G). Scanty, bald

=psegma, -to (G). Shavings

pselaph (G). Grope about, touch

pselli, -o, =um (G). A bracelet

psellism (G). Stammering

=psen (G). A fig insect

psen, -o (G). Bald

pseph, -i, -o (G). A small stone;
darkness

psephen, -o (G). Dark, obscure

psett, =a (G). A flatfish

pseud, -o (G). False

psil, -o (G). Bare, naked

psithyr, -o (G). Whispering

psitt, -ac, =acus (G). A parrot

=psoa (G). The loin; a muscle of the
loin

psoc (G). Rub small

psol, -o (G). Smoke, soot; one
circumcised

psom, -o, =us (G). A morsel

psoph, -o, =us (G). A sound, noise

psor, =a, -i, -o (G). Itch; scabies

psorale, -o (G). Scurfy

psych, =e, -i, -o (G). The soul,
mind; cold; a butterfly

psychr, -o (G). Cold

psydra, -c, =x (G). A pimple,
blister

psygm, =a, -ato, -o (G). Anything
that cools; chilliness

psyll, =a, -i, -o (G). A flea

psyxi, =s (G). A cooling

ptaer, -o (G). Sneeze

ptarm, -ic, -o (G). Sneezing, causing to sneeze

ptele, =a, -o (G). The elm

pten, -o (G). Feathered, winged

pter, -o, =um (G). A wing; a
feather; a fin

pteri, -do, =s (G). A fern

ptery, -g, -go, =x (G). A wing; a
feather; a fin

pteryl, -o (NL). A wing, feather

ptes, -i, -io (G). Flying

ptil, -o, =um (G). Down; a feather,
wing

ptilin, =um (NL). A wing-like membrane

ptin (NL). Feathered

ptis (G). Peel

pto, -s, -t (G). Fall

ptoch, -o (G). A beggar; crouch

=ptoma, -to (G). A fall; a corpse

ptorth, -o, =us (G). A sapling

ptos, =is (G). A fall, falling

ptot (G). Fall

pty, -ch, -ct, -g, -gm (G). Fold

ptya, -l, -li, -lo (G). Spit, spittle, saliva

ptych, -o (G). A fold

ptyct, -o (G). Folded

ptyg, -m, =ma, -mat, -o (G). Folded; a fold

ptyn, -g, =x (G). The eagle owl

ptyon, -o (G). A fan

=ptysma, -to (G). Spittle

ptyss, -o (G). Fold

ptyx, -i (G). Fold, folding

puber (L). A ripe age, adult; downy

=pubes (L). The hair appearing at puberty; the pubes

pubesc (L). Downy

pubi, -o; pubo (L). The region of the pubes

pud, -en, -i, -ic (L). Be ashamed; bashful

pudend, =um (L). The external female genitals; shameful

puell, =a (L). A girl

=puer, -i (L). A boy

pueril (L). Childish

puerper, -i (L). Childbearing

puffin, =us (NL). The puffin

=pugil, -i (L). A boxer

pugill, =us (L). A handful

=pugio, -n (L). A dagger

pugn, -a, -ac, =ax (L). Fight; fighting

pugn, -o, =us (L). The fist

pul, =ex, -ic (L). A flea

pulch, -ell, =er, -r (L). Beautiful

pull, =us (L). Dusky, dark-colored; a young fowl

pullari, =us (L). A chicken keeper

pullul, -a (L). Produce young, sprout

=pulmo, -n, -no (L). A lung

pulp, =a, -i (L). Flesh, pulp

puls, -a, -i, -ilo, -o (L). Beat, push, pulse

pult (L). Hurl, beat, knock

pult, -i (L). Pottage

pulv, -er, =is (L). Powder, dust

pulvi, -ll, -n (L). A cushion

pum, =ex, -ic (L). A soft stone

pumil, -io, -o (L). A dwarf

punct, -i (L). A sting, prick

punctat (L). Marked with pricks or punctures

pung, -en (L). Prick; penetrating

puni, -t (L). Punish

punic (L). Purple; reddish

punic, =a (L). The pomegranate

pup, =a, -i (L). A doll; a pupa

pupill, =a, -i (L). The pupil of the eye; a little girl

pur, -i (L). Pure; pus

purg, -a (L). Cleanse

puro (L). Pure; pus, inflammation

purpur, -e (L). Purple

puru (L). Pus, inflammation

-pus (G). A foot

=pus (L). Pus, inflammation

pusill (L). Very small

pusillanim (L). Faint-hearted

pustul, =a (L). A pimple, blister

put, -a (L). Prune, trim

putam, =en, -in (L). A husk, pod

putill, =us (L). A little boy

=putor, -i (L). A stench

putr, -e, -i (L). Rotten, putrid

py, -e, -o (G). Pus
pycn, -o (G). Thick, dense
pyct, =es (G). A boxer
pyel, -o, =us (G). A trough; the
  pelvis
pyg, =a, -o (G). The rump
pygarg, =us (L). A kind of eagle;
  a kind of antelope
pygm (G). A fist; boxing; the
  distance from the elbow to the
  knuckles (about 13½ inches);
  a dwarf
pyl, =a, =e, -o (G). A gate, ori-
  fice
pylor, -o, =us (G). A gate-keeper;
  the pylorus
pyo (G). Pus, inflammation
=pyosis (G). Pus formation
pyr, -i, =um, =us (NL). A pear
=pyr, -i, -o (G). Fire
pyr, =um (G). Wheat
pyrali, -d, =s (G). An insect
  fabled to live in fire
pyramid, -a (G). A pyramid;
  shaped like a pyramid
=pyren, -o (G). A fruit stone
pyret, -i, -o (G). Fever; fire
pyrexi (G). Fever; fire
pyrg, -o, =us (G). A tower
pyri (G): Fire; (NL): a pear
pyrin, -o (G). Of fire; of wheat
pyro (G). Fire; wheat
pyrrh, -o (G). Red, reddish;
  orange-colored
pyrrhic (G). A war dance
pyrrhul, =a (L). A bullfinch
pyrul, =a (NL). A pear
=pyrum (G): Wheat; (NL): a pear
=pyrus (NL). A pear
pyth, -o (G). Rot, decay
=python, -i, -o (G My). A serpent,
  python

=pyx (G). The rump
pyxi, -d, =s (G). A box

Q

quadr, -a, -i (L). Four
quadragesim (L). The fortieth
quadrat, -o (L). Square
quali (L). What kind
quant (L). How much
quart, -i, -o (L). A fourth
quasi (L). Nearly, almost, as
  though
quass, -at (L). Shaking, shaken
quatern (L). By fours
quatr, -i (L). Four
quer, -e, -i (L). Complain
querc, -i, =us (L). The oak
quern (L). Of oak, oaken
querquedul, =a (L). A kind of duck
questu, =s (L). A complaint
quie, -sc, -t (L). Quiet, resting
quin, -a, -i, -qu (L). Five
quin, =a, -i, -o (Sp). Quina bark
quincun, -c, =x (L). Five twelfths
quinqu, -e (L). Five
quint, -i, -o (L). Fifth
quis (L). What
quisc, -al, -ul (LL). A quail
quondam (L). Formerly
quot (L). How many

R

r (see also rh)
rab, -i, -o (L). Dark-colored
rabi, -d, =ies, -os (L). Mad, raving;
  rage, madness
racem, -i, -o, =us (L). A cluster
rachi, =a (G). A rocky shore; surf
rachi, -a, -o, =s (G). A spine; the
  backbone
radi, -a, -at, -o (L). A spoke, ray,
  radius

radian (L). Shining
radic, -a, -i, -l, -ul (L). A root
=radio (L). Ray; wireless; the
  radius of the arm
=radix (L). A root
radul, =a (L). A scraper
rai, =a (L). A skate, flatfish
rall, -i, =us (NL). A rail; thin
ram, =ex, -ic (L). A rupture
ram, -i, -o, =us (L). A branch
rament (L). Shreds, chips
rampan (F). Creeping, climbing
ran, =a, -i (L). A frog
ranc, -en, -id (L). Sour, putrid
=rangifer (NL). A reindeer
ranuncul, =us (L). A medicinal
  plant; a tadpole
rap, =a, -i (L). A turnip
rapa, -c, =x (L). Grasping,
  greedy
raph, =a (G). A seam, suture
raphan, -o, =us (G). A radish;
  a cabbage
raphi, -d, -o (G). A needle
rapi (L). A turnip
rapid (L). Tearing away; swift
rapt, -i, -o (G). Sewed
rapt, =or, -u (L). Seize, plunder;
  a plunderer
rar, -e, -i (L). Rare
rascet (L). The palm of the hand
rasi, -l (L). Scraped
rastr, -at, -i (L). Rake; with
  longitudinal scratches
rati, =o, -on (L). Rate, proportion
rati, =s, -t (L). A raft, flat-
  bottomed boat
rauc (L). Hoarse
rav, -i, -id (L). Tawny
re (L). Back, again
recept (L). Receive; a receiver
recidiv (L). Falling back, back-
  sliding

recipi (L). Receive
reciproc (L). Move back and forth
recit (L). Read out
reclinat (L). Bent back
reclus (L). Shut up
recondit (L). Concealed
rect, -i, -o (L). Straight; the rectum
recumben (L). Lying down
redact (L). Restored
redol (L). Emit a scent
redund (L). Overflow; abundant
reduvi, =a (L). A hangnail
reg, -al, -i (L). A king; royal
regim, =en, -in (L). Guidance
=regma, -to (G). A break, tear
regin, =a (L). A queen
regn (L). Rule, reign
regula, -ri, -t (L). Regular
=regulus (L). A little king, a prince
relict (L). Left behind
rem, =ex, -ig (L). A rower
rem, -i, =us (L). An oar
remedi (L). A cure
reminisc (L). Remember
remor, =a (L). Delay; a kind of fish
remulc, =um (L). Drooping; a tow
  rope
=remus (L). An oar
=ren, -a, -cul, -i, -o (L). A kidney
reniten (L). Resisting
repand (L). Turned up, bent backward
repen, -t (L). Creeping
repeti (L). Repeat
repl, =um (L). A door frame, bolt
replet (L). Full
replic (L). Fold back
rept, -a, -il (L). Creep, crawl
reptil, -i (L). Creep, crawl; a
  reptile
=res (L). A thing
resect (L). Cut off

resed, =a (L). Heal, calm; a kind
of plant

resid, -en (L). Live; remain
behind

resid, -i (L). Remaining; inactive

residu (L). What is left behind

resin, =a, -i (L). Resin

respir (L). Breathe

resplenden (L). Glittering

restan (L). Standing still

resti, =s (L). A rope, cord

restor (L). Put back again

resupin (L). Bent back

resuscita (L). Revive

ret, =e, -i, -in (L). A net,
network

retiari, =us (L). A net-fighter

reticen (L). Silent

reticul, -ari (L). A network

retin, -a, -i, -o (L). A net; the
retina of the eye

retin, =a, -i, -o (G). Pine resin

retinacul, =um (L). A holdfast

retr, -o (L). Back, behind, backward

retus (L). Blunt

revela (L). Reveal

revolut (L). Rolled back

=rex (L). A king

rh (see also r)

rhabd, -o, =us̄ (G). A rod

rhac, -o, =us (G). Rags

rhachi, =a (G). A rocky shore;
surf

rhachi, -a, -o, =s (G). The spine,
backbone

rhachist, -o (G). Cut up

rhadin, -o (G). Slender, delicate

rhaeb, -o (G). Crooked

rhag, -a, =e, -i, -o (G). Break,
break out, broken; a grape, berry

rhagi, -o, =um (G). A kind of spider

=rhagia (G). A breaking out

rhamn, -o, =us (G). Buckthorn

rhamph, -id, =is, -o (G). A curved
beak; a hook

rhani, -d, =s (G). Drop, sprinkle

rhaph, =a, -o (G). A seam, suture

rhaphan, -o, =us (G). A radish; a
cabbage

rhaphi, -d, -o, =s (G). A needle

rhapi, -do, =s (G). A rod, stick

=rhax (G). A grape, berry

rhe, =a (NL). A kind of bird

rhe, =a, -o (G). A flow, current

rhe, =um (ML). Rhubarb

rheb, -o (G). Crooked

rhect, -i (G). Rupture

rheg, =ma, -n (G). A break

rheithr, -o, =um (G). A stream

=rhema, -to (G). A word

rheo (G). A flow, current

rhest, -o (G). Destroyed

rhet, -i, -or (G). Speak

rhetin, =a, -i, -o (G). Pine resin

=rheum (NL). Rhubarb

rheum, =a, -ato, -i, -o (G). A
watery flow, flux

rhexi, -a, =s (G). A break, rupture

rhig, -o (G). Frost; shiver

rhin, =a (G). A shark; a file, rasp

rhin, -o (G). A nose

rhipi, -do, =s (G). A fan

rhips (G). Wickerwork

rhipt, -o (G). Thrown out

=rhis (G). A nose

rhiz, =a, -o (G). A root

rhod, -o, =um (G). A rose

rhoea, -d, =s (G). A kind of poppy

rhoec, -o (G). Crooked; failing,
weak

rhoga, -d, =s (G). Rent, ragged

rhomb, -o, =us (G). A parallelo-
  piped with equal sides; a top
rhonch, -o (G). Snore
rhop, -i, -o, =s (G). Bushes,
  brush
rhop, -o (G). A turning point,
  a turn of the scales
rhopal, -o, =us (G). A club
rhoph (G). To swallow
rhopo (G). Small, weak; bushes,
  brush; a turning point
=rhops (G). Bushes, brush
rhopt, -o (G). Absorption
rhoptr, -o, =um (G). A club
=rhus (L). Sumac
rhya, -co, =x (G). A stream
=rhyma, -to (G). Deliverance;
  defense
rhymb, -o, =us (G). Whirling; a
  top
rhynch, -o, =us (G). A snout, beak
rhyo (G). A stream
rhyp, -ar, -i, -o (G). Dirt, filth;
  filthy
rhyph, -o (G). Crooked; gulp
  down
rhypt (G). Cleanse
rhysi, =s (G). A stream; defend-
  ing
rhyss, -o (G). Wrinkled
rhythm, -o (G). Rhythm
rhyti, -do, =s (G). A wrinkle
rhytism, =a (G). A patch, darn
rhyz, -o (G). A root; growl
=ribes (Ar). A plant with sour sap
ricin, =us (L). Castor oil; the
  castor oil plant; a kind of tick
rict (L). Open-mouthed
rid, -e, -en (L). Laugh
ridicul (L). Laughable, funny
rig, -esc, -id, -or (L). Stiff,
  stiffening, harsh

rim, =a, -o (L). A fissure, split
ring, -en (L). Gape
rino (G). A nose
rip, =a, -ar, -i (L). The bank of
  a stream
ripi, -do, =s (G). A fan
ris, -or (L). Laugh, laughter
=rissa (Ice). The kittiwake
ritu, =s (L). A rite, ceremony
riv, -os, -ul (L). A brook, furrow
rival, -i (L). Of a brook; a rival
rob, -or, -ust (L). Strong; an oak
rod, -en (L). Gnaw, gnawing
rodo (G). A rose
roga (L). Ask
romale, -o (G). Strong-bodied
ror, -id, -ul (L). Dew, dewy
ros, =a (L). A rose
roscid (L). Dewy, wet
rose, -a, -o (L). Rose-colored,
  rosy
rosi (L). Gnaw
=rosmar (Dan). A walrus
=rosor (L). A gnawer
rostell, =um (L). A little beak
rostr, =um (L). A beak, snout;
  the prow of a ship
=rota, -li, -t (L). A wheel; revolve
rotund (L). Round
rub, -e, -i, =us (L). A bramble; a
  blackberry
rube, -d, -din, -o, =r, -scen (L).
  Red, reddish
rubi, -d, -g (L). Red, reddish
rubicund (L). Very red
rubicundul (L). Somewhat ruddy
rubigin (L). Rusty
rubr, -i (L). Red, reddish
=rubus (L). A bramble; a blackberry
ruct (L). Belch
rud, -eri, =us (L). Rubbish

ruden (L). Crying out, bellowing
rudi (L). Wild, rough
ruf, -esc, -i (L). Red, reddish
rug, ═a, -os, -ul (L). A wrinkle,
  fold; wrinkled
rum, ═a, -i (L). A dart
rum, ═en, -in (L). The throat
rum, ═ex, -ic (L). Sorrel
rumina (L). Chew the cud
rumor (L). Talk, hearsay
rump (L). Burst
runcin, ═a, -i (L). A carpenter's
  plane
rup, ═es, -estr, -i (L). A rock
rup, -i, ═ia, -o (G). Filth
rupinsulens (L). Of Rock Island
rupt (L). Broken, bursted
rur, -a, -i (L). The country; in
  the country
═rusa (Mal). A deer
rusc, ═um (L). A butcher's
  broom
russ (L). Reddish
rustic (L). Of the country
rut, ═a (L). A rue; disagree-
  ableness
ruthen (N). A province in Russia
ruti (G). A wrinkle
rutil (L). Red
rutr, ═um (L). A spade, shovel
rynch, -o, ═us (G). A beak,
  snout

S

sa, o (G). Healthy, safe
sab, -ell, -ul, -urr (L). Sand
sac, -o, ═us (G). A shield
sacc, -i, -o, ═us (L). A sack
sacchar, -o (G). Sugar
═sacer (L). Sacred
sacerdo, -t (L). A priest
saco (G). A shield

sacr, -a, -i (L). Sacred
sacr, -o, ═um (NL). The sacrum
sact, -o (G). Stuffed
═sacus (G). A shield
saenur, -id (G). Wag the tail
saep, ═es, -i (L). A fence
saffr (ME). Yellow
sag, -o (G). A covering, armor
saga, -c, ═x (L). Keen, shrewd
sagapen (L). A gum
sagar, -i (G). A sword
sage (G). Armor, harness
sagen, ═a (G). A seine
sagi, -do, ═s (G). A pouch
sagitt, ═a (L). An arrow
═sagma, -to (G). A pack saddle
sago (G). A covering, armor
═sal, -i (L). Salt
sal, -o (G). A roadside; restlessness
sala, -ci, ═x L). Lustful
salamandr, ═a (G). A salamander
salari (L). Of salt
salebr, -a, -os (L). Rough, uneven
sali (L). Salt; leap
sali, -ci, ═x (L). A willow
salien, -t (L). Leaping
salin (L). A salt pit; of salt,
  salty
salit, -an (L). Dancing, leaping
saliv, ═a (L). Spittle
═salix (L). A willow
═salmo, -n (L). The salmon
salo (G). A roadside; restlessness
salp, ═a, -i (L). A kind of sea fish
salpin, -ct, -g, -go, ═x (G). A
  trumpet
sals (L). Salted
salt, -a, -i (L). Leap, dance
saltator (L). A leaper, dancer
saltu, ═s (L). A forest

salu, -bri, -ti (L). Health; health-
   ful
salv, -a (L). Save, preserve
salvi, =a (L). The sage
samar, =a, -i (L). An elm seed
sambuc, =a (L). A stringed instrument
sambuc, =us (L). The elder tree
samyd, =a (G). A birch-like plant
sana, -b, -t (L). Heal, cure
sanct, -i (L). Saintly, holy
sandal, -o, =um (G). A sandal; a
   flatfish
sangui, -ni, =s (L). Blood
sanit, -a (L). Health, soundness
sanicul, =a (NL). A kind of plant
sani, -do, =s (G). A board, plank
santal, =um (NL). Sandalwood
sao (G). Healthy, safe
saperd, =es (G). A salted fish
saph, -en, -o (G). Clear, ap-
   parent; the truth
sapid (L). Tasty, savory
sapien, =s, -t (L). Wise, knowing
sapinda (L). Soapberry
=sapo, -ni (L). Soap
=sapor, -i (L). Flavor, taste
sapot, =a (NL). A kind of tree
sapphir, -o (G). The sapphire;
   blue
sapr, -o (G). Rotten, putrid
sarc, -i, -o (G). Flesh
sarcas, -m (LL). Sneer
sarcin, =a, -i (L). A bundle
sarcolip, =es (G). Lean, with
   little flesh
sarcopt (G). Flesh-cutting
sard, =a (G). A kind of fish
sarg, -o, =us (G). A kind of fish
sargass (Sp). Seaweed
sarment, =um (L). Twigs,
   branches

=saron, -to (G). A broom
sarp, -t (L). Prune, trim
sarri (L). Hoe, cultivate
sarsa (Sp). A bramble
sartori, =us (L). A tailor
=sarum (G). A broom
=sarx (G). Flesh
satan (G). The Devil, Satan
satell, =es, -it (L). An attendant
sathr, -o (G). Decayed, weakened
satur, -a (L). Full, filled
satyr (G My). A woodland deity, a
   satyr
sauci (L). Hurt, injured, ill
saucr, -o (G). Beautiful, graceful
saur, -o, =us (G). A lizard
savanna (Sp). A meadow
sax, -i, -o, =um (L). A rock
saxatil (L). Living among rocks
scab (L). Scratch, scrape
scab, =er, -r (L). Rough
scabell, =um (L). A footstool
scabi, =es (L). Itch, mange
scabios (L). Scaly, rough
scabr, -i (L). Rough
scae, -o (G). Clumsy; unlucky; on
   the left
scaer, -o (G). Dance
scal, =a, -ari, -i (L). A ladder
scalen, -e, -o (G). Uneven; limping
scali, -d, =s (G). A hoe; a bowl
scalm, -o, =us (G). An oar pin
scalma (OHG). Pestilence
scalop, -o, =s (G). A mole
scalp (L). Carve, scrape
scalpr, -i, =um (L). A chisel, knife
scalpt (L). Carved, scraped
scamb, -o (G). Curved, bent
scamill, =us (L). A little bench
scamn, -o, =um (L). A bench, stool
scan, -d, -s, -sor (L). Climb
scan, -i, -o, =us (G). A corpse

scap, =us (L): A stem; (G): a
  staff
scapan, -e, -i, -o (G). A spade
scaph, -i, -o (G). A bowl, boat,
  trough; anything hollowed out
scapt, =es, -o (G). Dig; a digger;
  dug out
scapul, =a (L). The shoulder blade
scar, =us (G). A kind of fish
scarabae, -i, =us (L). A scarab
  beetle
scari, -d, =s (G). A little worm
scarlatin (It). Scarlet
scart (G). Nimble; dance
=scarus (G). A kind of fish
scat, -o (G). Dung
scel, -i, -id, =is, -o, =us (G).
  A leg
sceler (L). Wicked, villainous
sceli, -do, =s (G). A leg; a rib
=scelio, -n (L). A scoundrel
scelo; =scelus (G). A leg
scen, -a, -o (G). A tent; a stage
sceptic, -o (G). Reflective, observant
sceptr, =um (L). A sceptre
sceu, -o, =us (G). An implement,
  vessel, equipment
schadon, -o (G). A bee larva;
  the honeycomb
sched, -o (G). A tablet
schedon (G). Near
sches, =is (G). A condition or
  state
=schema, -t, -to (G). Form, shape
scher, -o (G). One after another
schid, -i, =ium, -o (G). A
  splinter
schism, =a, -at, -o (G). A split-
  ting, division
schist, -o (G). Split, divided
schiz, -o (G). Split, cleave

schoen, -i, -o (G). A reed; a rope
=schola (L): School; (G): leisure
sci, -a, -o (G). A shadow
sciad, -i (G). A canopy, umbel
sciaen, =a (L). A sea fish
sciar, -o (G). Dark-colored, shady
=sciasma, -to (G). A shadow
sciatic (ML). Of the hip
scien, =s, -t (L). Knowledge
scier, -o (G). Dark-colored, shady
scill, =a (L). A sea onion
scinc, -i, =us (L). A kind of lizard
scintill (L). Emit sparks, sparkle
scio (G). A shadow
scirp, =us (L). A bulrush
scirrh, -o, =us (G). A tumor; a
  hard covering
scirt, -et, -o (G). Leap; a leaper
sciss, -i (L). Cut, split
scissur, =a (L). A fissure, cleft
sciur, -o, =us (L). A squirrel
scler, -o (G). Hard
scobi, =s (L). Sawdust, filings
scobin, =a (L). A rasp
scol, -o, =us (G). A thorn
scole, -c, =x (G). A worm
scoli, -o (G). Curved, crooked
scolop, -o, =s (G). Anything
  pointed; a stake
scolopa, -c, =x (G). A snipe
scolopendr, =a (G). A centipede
=scolus (G). A thorn
scolyt, -i (G). Clip, shorten
scomb, =er, -r (L). A mackerel
scop, =a (L). A broom; twigs
scop, =e, -o (G). See, watch, look
scopae, -o, =us (G). A dwarf
scopel, -o, =us (G). A cliff, high
  rock
scopi, scopo (G). A lookout, watch;
  a watch tower
=scops (G). An owl

scopt (G). Mock, jest, jeer
scopul, =a (L). A small broom
scopul, =us (L). A rock, crag
scopy (G). Observation
=scor, -a, -ia (G). Dung
scorbut, =us (ML). Scurvy
scord, -o, =um (G). Garlic, onion
scorod, =um (G). Garlic, onion
scorpaen, =a (G). A fish with a
  poisonous sting
scorpi, -o, =us (G). A scorpion
=scorpio, -n (L). A scorpion
scorzo (It). The adder
scot, -ia, -o, =us (G). Darkness
screa, -t (L). To hawk; split
scri, -b, -pt (L). Write
scrob, -i, =is (L). A trench
scrophul, -ari (L). A tumor,
  glandular swelling
scrot, =um (L). A pouch
scrup, -e, -os, -ul, =us (L).
  A rough or sharp stone
scrut, -at (L). Examine
sculpt (L). Carved
scut, -i, =um (L). A shield
scutell, =a (L). A dish
scutell, =um (L). A little shield
scybal, -o, =um (G). Dirt, filth,
  dung
scydmaen (G). Angry
scyla, -co, =x (G). A dog, puppy
scyll (G). A sea monster; mangle;
  vex, annoy; a dog, puppy
scyllar, =us (G). A kind of crab
scylo (G). Booty; an animal skin
scymn, -o, =us (G). A young
  animal, a whelp
scyph, -o, =us (G). A cup
scyr, -o (G). Rough
scyt, -i, -o (G). Leather; the neck
scytal, =a, -i, -o (G). A staff; a
  message

scythi (G N). To scalp
scythr, -o (G). Sullen, gloomy
scyti, scyto (G). Leather; the neck
seb, -i, =um (L). Grease, tallow
sebas, -m, -t (G). Venerable;
  reverent
sec, -o (G). A pen, enclusure; a
  shrine
seclu, -d, -s (L). Shut off, hidden
secret (L). Set apart, secret
sect (L). Cut
secund (L). The second, next
secur, -i, =is (L). An axe
=secutor (L). A follower, pursuer
sed, -ent, -i (L). Sit, sitting
sedat (L). Soothed, calm
sedit (L). A going aside
seduc (L). Lead aside, lead astray
sedul (L). Busy, diligent
=sedum (L). Stonecrop
sege, =s, -t (L). A corn field
segestr, =e, -i (L). A covering,
  wrapping
segm, -ent (L). A piece cut off
segn, -i (L). Slow, sluggish
segreg (L). Separate, set apart
sei, -o (G). Move to and fro, shake
seir, -o (G). A band, chain; hot
seism, -o, =us (G) A shaking, an
  earthquake
seiur (G). Wag the tail
sejug, -i (L). A six-horse team
sejunct (L). Separated
seko (G). A pen, enclosure; a
  shrine
sela, -sm, -t (G). Bright, shining
selach, -o, =us (G). A shark
selag, -in, =o (L). A kind of club
  moss
selen, -e, -i (G). The moon
seleni (NL). Selenium
seli, -d, =s (G). A plank, sheet

selin, =um (G). Parsley

sell, =a, -i (L). A saddle, stool

sema, -t, -to (G). A mark, sign, signal, seal

semae, -o (G). A standard, s streamer

semant, -o (G). Marked, significant

semasi (G). A marking

semat, -i, -o (G). A mark, sign, signal, seal

semeio, -t (G). Marked; a standard

=semen (L). Seed, sperm

semi (L). Half

semicincti, =um (L). An apron

semin, -i (L). Seed, sperm, semen

semn, -o (G). Holy, sacred

semo (G). A sign, mark, signal; a standard, streamer; a seal

semper (L). Always

sen, =ex, -i (L). An old person

sen, -i (L). Six

senari (L). Six each

senect (L). Very old, aged

senesc (L). Grow old

seni (L). An old person; six

senicul, =us (L). An old man

senil, -i (L). Of old people

sens, -i (L). Feeling

sensor (L). A sense organ

sent, -i (L). Feeling

senti, =s (L). A thorn

sep, -s, -t (G). Rotten, putrid

sepedo, -n (G). Rottenness, decay

sepi (L). Fence in

sepi, =a (G). A cuttlefish

seps (G). Rotten, putrid; a lizard

sepsi, =s (G). Putrid; putrefaction

sept, -em, -en (L). Seven

sept, -i, -o (G). Rotten, putrid; rot

sept, -i, -o, =um (L). A fence

septen, =ari (L). Seven each

septendecim (L). Seventeen

septentrion, -al (L). Northern

septi (L): A fence; (G): rotten

septim (L). The seventh

septo (L): A fence; (G): rot, rotten

septuagesi (L). The seventieth

septuagint (L). Seventy

=septum (L). A fence

sequa, -c, =x (L). Following

sequest, =er, -r (L). An agent, go-between

ser (L). Late

ser, -i, -o, =um (L). Whey, serum

seran, -g, =x (G). A cave

serapi, -ado, =as (G). An orchid

seren (L). Clear, calm, bright

seri (L). A series, row; late; Chinese; silk; serum

seri, -do, =s (G). Chicory, succory

seric, -a, -ar, -e, -o (G). Silk, silken

=sermo, -n (L). A speech

sero (L). Serum; late

serotin (L). Late

serp (L). Creep

serpent, -ar, -i (L). A serpent

serph, -o, =us (G). A gnat

serpul, =a, -o (L). A little snake

serr, =a, -at, -i (L). A saw

sert (L). Entwined, joined

sert, =a (L). Garlands

=serum (L). Whey; the watery part of fluids

serv, =a, -i, =us (L). A slave; serve

=ses, -i (G). A moth

sesam, =e (G). Sesame

sesel, -i (G). A shrub
sesqui (L). One and one-half
sessil (L). Sitting on, sedentary,
  without a stem
sestr, -o, =um (G). A sieve
set, =a, -i (L). A bristle
set, -o (G). A moth
seth, -o, =us (G). A sieve
sever (L). Serious, harsh
sex, -a (L). Six
sexagesim (L). The sixtieth
sexagint (L). Sixty
sext (L). The sixth
sexu (L). Sex
si, -o (G). Move to and fro,
  shake
siag, -on (G). The jaw bone
sial, -i, -o (G). Spittle, saliva;
  fat, grease
siali, =s (G). A kind of bird
=sialum (G). Spittle, saliva
=sialus (G). Fat, grease
sibil (L). Hissing
sibyn, -e, -o (G). A spear
sicari, =us (G). An assassin
sicc (L). Dry
sicy, -o, =us (G). A gourd, cucumber
sid, =a (G). A pomegranate tree;
  a kind of water plant
sid, -eri, =us (L). A star
sider, -a, -o, =us (G). Iron
sidere (L). Starry
sig, =a, -o (G). Silence
sigill, =a, -o (L). A seal; the
  little figures on a seal
sigm, =a, -ato, -o (G). The
  letter "S"; S-shaped
sign, -i, =um (L). A sign, mark
sigo (G). Silence
sil, -o (G). Snub-nosed
sila, =us (L). A kind of parsley
silen, -t (L). Still, silent

silen, =us (L): Foam; (My): drunkenness
=silex (L). Flint
silic, -i (L). Flint
siliqu, =a (L). A pod, husk
sillo (G). Satire
silph, =a (G). A kind of beetle
silphi, =um (G). A plant with
  medicinal properties
silub, -o, =um (G). A kind of thistle
silur (L). A kind of fish; a region in
  South Wales
silv, =a, -at, -estr, -i (L). Woods,
  trees
silyb, -o, =um (G). A kind of thistle
sim, -o (G). Flat-nosed
simbl, -o, =us (G). A beehive
simi, =a, =us (L). An ape
simil (L). Alike, similar
simpl, =ex, -ic, -ici (L). Simple
simul (L). Together; imitate
simula (L). A likeness; imitate
sin, -a, -o (G). Chinese; damage
sinapi, =s (L). Mustard
sincip, -it, =ut (L). The forehead
sinens (NL). Of China
singul, -ar (L). Separate, solitary
sini, -o, =um (G). A sieve
sinist, =er, -r (L). The left hand;
  awkward; evil
sino (G). Chinese; damage
sinu, -a, -o, =s (L). A fold; a hollow;
  bend, wind
sio (G). Move to and fro, shake
sipal, -o (G). Deformed
siphl, -o (G). Crippled, maimed
siphn, -e, -o (G). A mole; crippled,
  blind
sipho, -n, -no (G). A tube, pipe
sir, =ex, -ic (G). A kind of wasp
siren, -i, -o (L My). A mermaid-
  like creature with an enticing
  voice

-sis (G). The act of
sistr, =um (L). A rattle
sisymbr, -i, =ium, -o (G). A
  sweet-smelling plant
sisyr, =a, -o (G). A garment of
  skin
sisyrinchi, =um (G). An iris-like
  plant
sit, -i, -io, -o, =us (G). Food
sit, -u, =us (L). A place
sitt, =a, -i (G). A nuthatch
=sium (G). A marsh plant
sk (see also sc)
skat, -o (G). Dung
skelet, -o (G). A dried body,
  skeleton
skelo (G). A leg
skeptic, -o (G). Reflective,
  observant
skia (G). A shadow
skiro (G). A white parasol
skler, -o (G). Hard
smaragd, -o (G). An emerald
smari, =s (G). A small sea fish
=smegma, -to (G). A soapy secretion; a cleansing substance
smerinth, -o, =us (G). A cord,
  string
smil, =a, -o (G). A carving knife
smila, -c, =x (G). Yew; bindweed
sminth, =us (G). A field mouse
smodi, -c, -ng, =x (G). A swollen
  bruise
sobar, -o (G). Arrogant; violent
sobol, =es, -i (L). A sprout, shoot
sobrin, =us (L). A cousin
soci, =a, -o, =us (L). A companion, fellow being, ally
sodal, -i, =is (L). A companion
=sol, =a (L). The sun
sol, -i, -o (L). Alone
sol, =um (L). The floor, bottom,
  earth

solan, -a, =um (L). A nightshade
solar, -i (L). Of the sun
sole, =a (L). A sandal; a kind of
  fish
solen, -i, -o (G). A pipe, channel
soli (L). The sun; alone
solic (L). Care, concern
solid (L). Dense, firm
solidag, -in, =o (L). Goldenrod
solitari (L). Solitary
solo (L). Alone
solpug (L). A venomous ant or
  spider
solu (L). Alone; dissolve
=solum (L). The floor, bottom,
  earth
solut, solv (L). Dissolved, loose
=soma, -t, -to (G). A body
somn, -i, =us (L). Sleep
somph, -o (G). Spongy, porous
son, -a, -it, -o (L). Sound
sonch, =us (G). A sow thistle
sonor, -o (L). Noisy
soph, -o (G). Wise, skillful
sophistic (G). Artful, shrewd
sophora (Ar). A kind of tree
sophron, -o (G). Temperate, sensible
-sophy (G). Wisdom, skill, art
=sopor, -i (L). Sleep
sor, -i, -o, =us (G). A heap
sorb (L). Suck in, absorb
sorb, -a, =us (L). A kind of tree
sord, -id (L). Filthy
=sorex (L). A shrew
sori (G). A heap
soric (L). A shrew
soro (G). A heap; a coffin
=soror, -i (L). A sister
sort, -i (L). Lot, fate
=sorus (G). A heap
sostr, -o (G). A reward for saving
  another's life

sot, -er, -eri (G). Preserve, save, deliver

soz, -o (G). Preserve, save, deliver

spad (G). Draw, draw off

spadi, -c, =x (G). A palm branch; brown

spadice (NL). Brown

spado, -n (G). A castrated individual

spala, -ci, -co, =x (G). A mole

span, -o (G). Lacking, scarce

spar, -i, =us (L). The gilt-bream

spara, -ct, -gm, -ss, -xi (G). Tear, mangle; torn, mangled

sparg (G): Swell, teem; (L): strew, scatter

spargan (G). A swath, bank; a kind of plant

spari (L). The gilt-bream

spars (L). Thin, scattered

spart, -e, -i, -o (G). A rope; a kind of plant

spart, -o (G). Scattered

=sparus (L). The gilt-bream

sparveri, =us (L). A sparrow

spasm, =a, -at, -o, =us (G). An involuntary muscular act, a convulsion

spastic (G). Relating to convulsions

spatang, =es (G). A sea urchin

spath, =a, -i, -o (G). A broad sword

spati, =um (L). A space

spatil, =a, -o (G). Excrement

spatul, =a (L). A little blade; a spoon

spe, -o (G). A cave

speci (L). A kind or sort, species; special; look at, see

specios (L). Showy, beautiful

spect (L). See, look at

spectabil (L). Visible, remarkable

spectr, -o (L). A sight; the spectrum

specu, =s (L). A cave or hole

specul, =a (L). A watch tower

specul, =um (L). A mirror

specula, -t (L). Search, examine

speir, -o (G). Coil; scatter

speis (G). Food

spel, -ae, -ea, -eo, -o (G). A cave

speo (G). A cave

sperg (NL). Scatter

sperm, =a, -at, -ato, -i, -o (G). Seed, semen, male reproductive cells

sphacel, -o, =us (G). Gangrene

sphadasm, -o, =us (G). A convulsion

sphaer, =a, -i, -o (G). A ball, sphere

sphag, =e, -i (G). The throat; slaughter, sacrifice

sphagn, =um (G). A kind of moss

sphaler, -o (G). Slippery, treacherous

spharag, -o (G). Noisy, sputtering

sphe, -ci, =x (G). A wasp

sphedan, -o (G). Violent, vehement

sphen, =a, -o (G). A wedge

spher, =a , -o (G). A ball, sphere

=sphex (G). A wasp

sphigm, -o (G). The pulse

sphin, -ct, -g, =x (G). Bind tight, squeeze, strangle; a mythological monster, the sphinx

sphodr, -o (G). Active, violent

sphrag, -i, =is (G). A seal, signet ring

sphrig, -o (G). Vigorous

sphygm, -o (G). The pulse

sphyr, -o (G). A hammer, mallet; the ankle

spic, =a, -ul (L). A spike, point; an ear of grain

spiegel (G). A mirror

spil, -o, =us (G). A spot, stain;
a cliff

spin, =a, -i (L). A spine, thorn

spinthar, -i, =is (G). A spark

=spinther, -o (G). A spark

=spinus (L). A linnet-like bird

=spio (L My). A sea nymph

spir, =a, -o (L). Breathe; a
spiral, coil

spirac, -l, -ul, =ulum (L). An air
hole

=spiraea (L). The meadowsweet

-spire (L). Breathe

spirem, =a, -at (G). A coil,
twisted thread

spiro (L). A spiral, coil; breathe

spiss, -a, -at, -i (L). Compact,
thickened

spiz, =a (G). A finch

splanchn, -i, -o, =um (G). The
viscera

=splen, -i, -ico, -o (G). The spleen;
a bandage, patch

spod, -i, -o (G). Ashes, slag; gray

=spolia, -t (L). Booty, spoils

spondyl, -o (G). A vertebra

spong, -i, =ia, -io, -o (G). A
sponge

=sponsa (L). A bride

spor, =a, -i, -o (G). A seed

sporad, -o (G). Scattered

spuda, -st (G). Haste, zeal;
active

spui (L). Spit

spum, =a (L). Foam

spurc (L). Dirty, filthy

spuri (L). False

sput, =um (L). Spittle

spyr, -id, -o (G). A basket

squal, =us (L). A dogfish

squalid (L). Foul, filthy

squalor (L). Dirt, filth

squam, =a, -at, -i, -o (L). A scale

squarros (L). Scaly, rough

=squatarola (It). The black-bellied
plover

squatin, =a (L). A skate

squill, =a, -i (L). A sea onion; a
shrimp

stabil, -i (L). Firm

stach, =ys (G). A spike, ear of corn

stact, -o (G). Trickling

stag, -eto, =ma, -mat, -mo (G). A
drop

stagn, -a, -i, =um (L). Motionless;
a pool

stala, -ct, -gm (G). Dripping, dropping

-stalsis (G). A constriction, compression

stalt (G). Constriction, compression

stam, =en, -in (L). Anything standing
upright; a thread; a stamen

stamn, -o (G). A wine jar

stann, -i, =um (L). Tin

stape, -di, =s (LL). A stirrup; the
stapes, a bone in the ear

staphi, =s (G). A raisin

staphyl, =a, -o (G). A bunch of grapes,
a cluster; the uvula

staphylin, =us (G). A kind of insect

starn (ME). A kind of bird

stas, -i, =is (G). Standing, posture

stat, -i, -o (G). Standing, placed

static, =e, -o (G). An astringent
herb

staur, -o, =us (G). A cross

staxi, =s (G). A dropping

stea, =r, -t, -to (G). Fat, suet,
tallow

stechi, -o (G). An element

steg, -an, -ano, -no, -o (G). A
cover, roof; covered

steir, -o (G). Sterile; a keel

stel, =a, -id, -o (G). A pillar

stele, -o (G). A handle

stelgi, -do, =s (G). A scraper

stell, =a, -i, -o (L). A star

stelm, -a (G). A crown

stelo (G). A pillar

stem, -a, -o (G). A thread; a stamen

=stemma, -to (G). A crown, garland

sten, -o (G). Narrow

=stenosis (G). A narrowing, contraction

stentor (G My). A powerful voice; a trumpet

step (AS). Orphaned

steph, -ano, =anus, -o (G). A crown

stere, -o (G). Solid

sterc, -o, -or, =us (L). Excrement, dung, manure

steres, =is (G). Deprivation, loss

=sterigma, -to (G). A support

steril, -i (L). Barren, sterile

steriph, -o (G). Firm, solid

stern, -o, =um (G). The breast, breastbone

stern, =a (NL). A tern

sternu, -t (L). Sneeze

sterr, -ho, -o (G). Solid, stiff

stert (L). Snore

steth, -o, =us (G). The breast, chest

sthen, -ar, -o, =us (G). Strength, might

stib, =a, -i (G). Hoar frost; antimony

stib, -o, =us (G). A track, tread

stich, -o, =us (G). A row, line

stichari, =um (G). A vestment, tunic

stict, -o (G). Punctured, dappled

stig, -a (L). Goad, prick

stigm, =a, -at, -ato, -o (G). A spot; a brand; a pricking

stil, =a (G). A drop

stil, =us (L). A style; a stake

stilb (G). Glitter, glisten

still, =a, -ic (L). A drop

stilpn, -o (G). Glistening

=stilus (L). A style; a stake

stimul, -a, =us (L). Goad

stinct (L). Prick

=stipatio, -ni (L). A crowd

stipendi, =um (L). Tribute, payment

=stipes (L). A stalk, stem

stiphr, -o (G). Stout, sturdy

stipi, -ti (L). A stalk, stem

stipt, -o (G). Trodden down

stiri, =a (L). An icicle

stirp, -i, =s (L). A stock, stem

stixi, =s (G). A puncture

stiz, -o (G). Prick, puncture

=stoa (G). A porch

stoichi, -o (G). An element

stol, =a, -o (L). A long robe

stolid (L): Dull, stupid; (G): a robe

=stolo, -ni (L). A twig, shoot

stom, =a, -ato, -o (G). A mouth

stomach, -i, -o, =us (G). The gullet; the stomach

stomb, -o (G). Noisy

stomph, -ac, -o (G). Loud-talking

stomyl, -o (G). Talkative

stony, -cho, =x (G). A sharp point

storth, =a, -o, -yng (G). A point; the point of an antler

strab, -i, -ism, -o (G). Squint; squint-eyed, cross-eyed

strado (It). Street

stragul, =um (L). A cover, mantle

stram, =en, -in, -ine (L). Straw

stran, -g, =x (G). A drop

strang, -o (G). Crooked; squeeze
strangal (G). Choke
strangulat (L). Choked
strat, -age, -eg (G). Generalship
strat, -i, =um (L). A bed covering; a layer
strat, -io, -o (G). An army; a
soldier
strebl, -o (G). Twisted
=stremma, -to (G). A sprain, a
twisting
stren, -o (G). Strong, harsh;
haughty
strenu (L). Active
streper (LL). Noisy
streph, -o (G). Turn, twist
strepit, -an (L). Noisy
strepsi, =s (G). A turning or
twisting
strept, -o (G). Bent, twisted;
pliable
=stria, -t (L). A furrow, streak;
furrowed, streaked
strict (L). Drawn together, tight
strid, -en, -or, -ul (L). Creak,
make a harsh sound
strig, =a (L). A furrow, streak
strig, -i (L). An owl; a furrow
strigat (L). Streaked, striped
strigil, =is (L). A scraper
strigos (L). Thin, meager
stringen (L). Compressing
string (NL). An owl
striol, =a (L). A small furrow
=strix (L). An owl; a furrow
strob, -o (G). Twist, turn, whirl
strobil, -o, =us (G). Anything that
whirls; a top; a pine cone
=stroma, -t, -to (G). Anything
spread out; a coverlet, mattress,
bed

stromb, -i, -uli, =us (L). A spiral;
a snail; a top
strongyl, -o (G). Round
stroph, -i, -io, -o (G). A cord or
twisted band; turn, twist
struct (L). Build
strum, =a, -o (L). A tumor
=struthio, -n (L). An ostrich
strychn, -o, =us (G). A nightshade
stryphn, -o (G). Sour, harsh
stud, -en, -i (L). Be diligent; zeal
stult, -i (L). Foolish, silly
stup, =a, -o (L). The coarse part of
flax
stup, -e, -id (L). Benumb, stun
stupr (L). Defile, corrupt
=sturio, -n (LL). The sturgeon
sturn, -i, =us (L). A starling
styg, -ano, -er, -et, -no, -o (G).
Hatred; hated; hating
styl, -o, =us (G). A pillar, stake,
column; a pointed instrument
stym, -a (G). Stiff, erect
styp, -h, -t (G). Astringent
styp, -o, =us (G). A stump, stem
styphel, -o (G). Sour; tough
styphl, -o (G). Harsh; sour, astringent
styr, -ac, =ax, -o (G). A kind of
shrub
suas (L). Persuade
sub (L). Under, below
sub, =ex, -ic (L). An under layer,
support
=suber, -i (L). The cork oak
sublim (L). Uplifted, exalted
subruf, -i (L). Buff
subul, =a (L). An awl
succ, =us (L). Juice, sap
succin, -e, =um (L). Amber
succis (L). Cut, bitten off,
trimmed

such, -i, -o, =us (G). A crocodile
sucr, -o (F). Sugar
suct, -or (L). Suck; a sucker
sud, -a, =or, -ori (L). Sweat
sudi, =s (L). A stake; the pike
suecic (L). Swedish
suf (L). Under, below
sufflat (L). Puffed up, bloated
suffrag (L). Support; voting
  right
suffrag, -in, =o (L). The hock,
  pastern bone
sug (L). Suck
sui (L). Self; a pig
sul, =a, -i (Ice). A gannet
sulc, -a, -i, =us (L). A furrow,
  groove, trench
sulf, -o (L). Sulphur
sulph, -o (L). Sulphur
summ, =a (L). The sum, total
super (L). Above, over
supin (L). Lying on the back
supplic (L). Beg
suppra (L). Form pus
supra (L). Above, over, beyond
sur (F): Above; (L): calf of leg
surcul, =us (L). A twig, sprout
surd, -it (L). Deaf; deafness
surg (L). Rise, raise
=surnia (NL). The hawk owl
sursum (L). Above, upward
=sus (L). A pig
suscept (L). Undertake
susurr (L). Buzzing, whispering
sutil (L). Sewed together
sutur, =a (L). A seam
sy, -g, -l, -m, -n, -s (G). With,
  together
syba, -co, =x (G). Hog-like
sybari (G My). Lascivious; volup-
  tuary
sybot (G N). A swineherd

syc, -a, -i, -o, =um (G). A fig
sycamin, -o, =us (G). The mulberry
sychn, -o (G). Many
syg, syl (G). With, together
syllab (G). That which holds or is
  held together; a syllable
sylleg, -o (G). Gather
sylleps, =is (G). A putting together
sylli (NL). A necklace
syllog, -i, -o (G). A gathering together, reckoning
sylv, =a, -at, -estr, -i (L). Woods,
  forest
sym (G). With, together
symbio (G). Living together
symmetr (G). Suitable; symmetry
symp, -y (G). Squeeze together
sympher, -o (G). Useful
symphy, -o, -so (G). Growing together
symploc, -o (G). Connected, interwoven
symptom, -a, -ato, -o (G). A symptom
symptosi, =s (G). A meeting
syn (G). With, together
synap, -s, =sis, -t (G). A falling together, a union
syncop (G). Cut short, cut up
syndesm, -o, =us (G). A bond, ligament
synech, -i, -o (G). Hold together
synerg (G). Cooperate, work together
synesi, =s (G). A joining; understanding
synoch, -o (G). Meeting, joining
synost, -eo (G). A bone articula-
  tion
synul, -o (G). Healing, scar-form-
  ing
=syphar, -o (G). Wrinkled skin
syphil (G). Swine-loving
syphil, -i, -o (L). Syphilis

syrig, -m (G). Piping, whistling
syrin, -g, -go, =x (G). A pipe
syrm, =a, -ato, -o (G). Sweep-
  ings, refuse; something dragged
  along
syrph, -a, -ac, =ax, -et (G). Anything swept together, refuse;
  vulgar
syrph, -o, =us (G). A gnat
syrti, -do, =s (G). A sand bank
sys (G). With, together
sysci, -o (G). Shaded
systatic (G). Introductory
=systema, -t, -to (G). A system
systol, -o (G). A contraction
systom, -o (G). With a narrow
  mouth
systroph (G). Twist together,
  roll up
syzyg, -o (G). Yoked, paired

T

tab, -e, =id (L). Wasting away
tab, -l, -ul, =ula (L). A board,
  table
tabac, =um (NL). Tobacco
taban, =us (L). A horse fly
tabern (L). A shed, tent
tabe, =s, -t (L). Wasting away
tabid (L). Wasting away
tabul, =a (L). A board, table
tach, -eo (G). Quickly
tach, -in, -y (G). Swift, fast
tach, -o (G). Speed
tacit (L). Without words, silent
tact, -i (L). Touch
tadorn, =a (NL). A kind of duck
taedios (L). Disgusting
taeni, =a, -o (G). A band, ribbon
=tagma, -to (G). A division, a
  body of soldiers
tal, -ari, -i, -o, =us (L). The
  ankle, heel

tala, -n (G). Wretched
talaepor, -i (G). Toil; miserable
talant, -o, =um (G). A balance,
  scales
talar, -o, =us (G). A basket
talari, tali (L). The ankle, heel
talitr (L). Strike with the finger
talo (L). The ankle, heel
talp, =a (L). A mole
=talus (L). The ankle, heel
tamia, =s (G). A distributor
tana, -o (G). Stretched
tanacet, =um (OF). The tansy
tanagr (Br). A tanager
tang, -i (L). Touch
tann, =um (ML). Tanning
tany, -o (G). Stretch, stretched
tao, -n, =s (G). A peacock
tape, =s, -to (G). A carpet
tapein, -o (G). Low
taph, -o, -r (G). A burial; astonishment
taphr, -o, =us (G). A trench
tapin, -o (G). Low
tapir, -o (Sp). A tapir
tarac, -h, -t (G). Disorder; disturb
=taragma, -to (G). Trouble, uneasi-
  ness
tarand, =us (G). The reindeer
tarant (It). A town in Italy
taraxi, =s (G): Confusion, trouble;
  (Ar): a kind of succory
tarb, -o (G). Terror
tarbale (G). Fearful
tard, -i (L). Slow
tarph, -i, -o (G). A thicket
tarphy (G). Thick, close
tars, -o, =us (G). A flat surface;
  the ankle, tarsus
tas, -eo, -i (G). Stretching
tass (G). Arrange
-tatos (G). (the superlative ending)
taur, =us (L). A bull

taut, -o (G). The same
tax, -eo, -i, =is, -o (G). Arrange;
  arrangement
tax, -o, =us (G). Yew
tax, -o, =us (NL). A badger
tebenn, =a (G). A robe
tec, -o (G). Melt away
techn, -i, -o (G). Art, skill
tecn, -o, =um (G). A child
tect, -i, -o (L). A roof, covering
tect, -o (G): A carpenter, builder;
  soluble; (G): a roof, cover;
  covered
tector, -i (L). Plaster, stucco
tedi (L). Weary
teg, -o, =us (G). A roof
tegm, =en, -in (L). A cover
tegul, =a (L). A roof tile
teich, -o, =us (G). A wall
tein, -o (G). Extend, stretch
tekn, -o, =um (G). A child
tel, =a, -i (L). A web
tel, -e (G). Far
tel, -eo, -o (G). An end; complete
teleut (G). Completion, fulfill-
  ment
teli (L). A web
tellin, =a (G). A kind of shellfish
tellu, -r, -ri, =s (L). The earth
=telma, -to (G). A pond, pool
telo (G). An end; complete
=telson (G). A boundary
temen, =us (G). A piece of land
temer (L). Rash, reckless
temn, -o (G). Cut
temper (L). Moderate
templ, =um (L). An open space;
  a temple
tempor, -a, -o (L). Time; the
  temples
ten, -a (L). Hold

ten, -s, -t (L). Stretched
tena, -ci, =x (L). Holding fast, tough
tenag, -o, =us (G). A pool, shoal
tenan (L). Holding
tend, -in, -o (L): Stretch; a tendon;
  (G): gnaw
=tenebrio, -n (L). A lover of darkness
tenebros (L). Dark, gloomy
tenen (L). Holding
tener, (L). Tender, soft
tenesm, =us (G). A straining
teni, =a, -o (G). A band, ribbon
tenon, -t, -to (G). A tendon
tens, tent (L). Stretched
tenta (L). Handle, touch, feel
tentacul, -i, =um (LL). A feeler
tenthred, -in, =o (G). A kind of
  wasp
tentig, -in, =o (L). A stretching
tentori, =um (L). A tent
tenu, -i (L). Thin, slender
tep, -id, -or (L). Warm
tephr, -o (G). Ashes; ash-colored,
  gray
ter (L). Three; three times
tera, =s, -to (G). A wonder; a
  monster
teram, -no, -o (G). Soft
teramn, -o, =us (G). A closed room
terasti (G). Monstrous; portentious
tere, -no (G). Smooth, delicate
tere, -o (G). Bore, perforate;
  watch, guard
tere, =s, -t (L). Round, smooth
terebr, =a (L). Bore; a boring tool
terebinth, =us (G). The turpentine
  tree
tered, -o (G). A wood worm
tereno (G). Smooth, delicate
tereo (G). Bore, perforate; watch,
  guard

=teres, teret (L). Round, smooth
teretr, -o (G). A gimlet
terg, -i, =um (L). The back
teri (G). Pierce
-terium (G). A place for
=terma, -t (G). An end, limit
term, =es, -it (L). A wood worm
term, -in (L). An end; a name
termin, -a, =us (L). An end, limit
termin, -o, =us (ML). A term, name
termit (L). A wood worm
tern, -ari (L). Three; in threes
terph, -o, =us (G). A shell, covering
terpn, -o (G). Delightful
terps, -i (G). Delight, gladness
terr, =a, -i (L). The earth, land
terr, -i (L). Terror
terrestr (L). On land
ters (L). Clean, neat
terti (L). The third
tessar (G). Four; square
tesselat (L). Checkered
test, =a (L). A tile, shell
testac, -e (L). With a shell; of brick
testi =s (L). A witness; a testicle
testicul (L). Of the testes
testud, -in, =o (L). A turtle
tetan, -o, =us (G). Rigid, tense; tetanus
tetart, -o (G). The fourth
teth, -o, =us (G). An oyster
tethe (G). A grandmother
tetr, -a (G). Four
tetra, -c, =x (G). A pheasant
tetric (L). Harsh, stern
tetrig; =tetrix (G). A grouse
tetti, -g, =x (G). A grasshopper, cicada

teuch, -o, =us (G). An implement; a vessel
teuthi, =s (G). A squid
teutl, -o, =um (G). A beet
texi (G). Birth
text, -i (L). Weave
thair, -o, =us (G). A door hinge
thal, -o, =us (G). A twig; a young person
thalam, -i, -o, =us (G). A chamber, inner room
thalass, =a, -i, -o (G). The sea
thaler, -o (G). Fresh, blooming
=thalia (G My). Bloom; joy
thall, -o, =us (G). A young shoot, twig
thalo (G). A twig; a young person
thalp, -o (G). Heat
thalycr, -o (G). Hot, glowing
thamb, -o, =us (G). Astonishment
thamn, -o, =us (G). A shrub
thana, -s, -to, =tus (G). Death
=thapsia (G). A poisonous plant
thapsin, -o (G). Yellow
thapt, -o (G). Bury
=thauma, -si, -st, -to (G). A wonder; wonderful
the, =a, (G): A view, spectacle; (L): tea
the, -i, (G): A god; (L): tea
the, -o (G). Run; a god
theat, -r (G). An audience; a theatre
thec, =a, -o (G). A case, box, chest, cup
thect, -o (G). Sharpened
theg, -o (G). Sharpen
thei (G): Run; a god; (L): tea
thei, -o (G). Sulphur
thel, =a, -i (G). A nipple
thel, -y (G). Female; tender
thelasm, -o (G). Suck, suckle
thelic, -o (G). Feminine

thelx, -i (G). Bewitching
thely (G). Female; tender
-them (NL). Put
thema, -t (G). A thing laid down;
  a theme
themeli, =a (G). A foundation
=themis (G). Law, justice
=thenar, -o (G). The palm of the
  hand
theo (G). Run; a god
=theorema, -to (G). A spectacle;
  a theory
ther, -i, -io, =ium (G). A wild
  beast
ther, -o (G). Summer; hunt for
thera, -to (G). Hunting, pursuit
therap, -eu, -o, =y (G). Serve;
  treatment
theri, -a, -d, -o (G). A wild
  beast
therm, -o (G). Heat; a lupine
thero (G). A wild beast; summer;
  hunt for
thesaur, -i, -o (G). A treasure
=thesis (G). An arranging
thesm, -o, =us (G). A law, rule
thet (G). Place, arrange; a servant
theurg (G). Supernatural
thias, -o, =us (G). A band, company
thigm, =a, -ato, -o (G). A touch
thin, -o (G). The shore; a sand
  heap
thio, -n (G). Sulphur
thlas, -t (G). Crush, flatten
thlasp, =i (L). A kind of cress
thlib, -o (G). Press, squeeze
thlips, -i (G). Press, squeeze;
  pressure
tho, -o (G). Quick; a jackal
thol, -o, =us (G). A dome; mud

tholer, -o (G). Muddy
thomi, -ng, =nx, -s (G), A whip,
  string
thoo (G). Quick; a jackal
thor, -o (G). Rushing; the semen
=thora (LL). A bed
thora, -co, =x (G). A breastplate;
  the thorax
thorect, -o (G). Armed with a breastplate
thorict, -o (G). Armed with a breastplate
thoro (G). Rushing; the semen
=thorus (LL). A bed
thoryb, -o, =us (G). A noice, uproar
thran, -i, -o (G). A bench; a sword-
  fish
thras, -y (G). Bold
thrass, -o (G). Disturb
thraupi, =s (G). A small bird
thraust, -o (G). Brittle
=thremma, -to (G). A nursling
thren, -o (G). Wail, lament
threps, -i, -o (G). Nourishment
thrept (G). Feeding; nourished
thrida, -c, =x (G). Lettuce
thrina, -c, =x (G). A three-pronged
  fork
thrinc, -o, =us (G). A cornice, eaves
thrip, -i, -o, =s (G). A wood worm
=thrix (G). Hair
thromb, -o, =us (G). A clot, blood
  clot
throsc, -o (G). Spring, leap
thry, -o, -on (G). A rush, reed
thryp, -si, -t (G). Break in pieces;
  crushing
=thuja (ML). Arbor vitae
=thula (Ch). The snowy egret
thunn, =us (L). The tunny fish
thur, =a (G). A door
thur, -i (L). Incense

thurid (G). Rushing, impetuous

thuy, =a (G). Arbor vitae

thyell, =a, -o (G). A hurricane

thylac, -o (G). A sack, pouch

thym, -o, =us (G). The mind,
  spirit, courage; rage; thyme; the
  thymus gland

thymall, =us (G). A kind of fish

thymel (G). An altar, a place of
  sacrifice; scenic

thymiama (G). Incense; burn

thymo; =thymus (G). The mind,
  spirit; rage; thyme; the thymus
  gland

thynn, =us (G). The tunny fish

thyo (G). A sacrifice; incense

thyr, =a, -i, -o (G). A door

thyr, -eo (G). A shield

thyri, -do, =s (G). A window

thyrs, -o (G). A wand or staff

thysan, -o, =us (G). A fringe

tiar, =a, -o (G). A headdress

tibi, =a, -o (L). The shin bone

tibic, =en, -in (L). A flute player

-tic (G): Relation; (L): belonging to

tich, -o (G). A wall

tigill, =um (L). A piece of wood

tign, =um (L). A beam, timber

tigri, -n (L). A tiger; striped like
  a tiger

=tilia (L). The linden tree

till, -o (G). Tear, pull out

tilt, -o (G). Plucked

tim, -id, -or (L). Fear

tim, =a, -o (G). Honor, esteem

timi, -o (G). Valued, precious

timor (G): Avenge; (L): fear

tin, -o (G). Stretch, extend;
  punish

=tinagma, -to (G). An agitation

tinct (L). Dyed, tinged

tine, =a, -i (L). A moth

tinn, -it, -ul (L). Ringing, tinkling

tino (G). Stretch, extend; punish

tintinn (L). Ring, jingle

tintinnabul, =um (L). A bell

tinto (It). Tint

tiph, =a, -i (G). A kind of insect

tipul, =a (L). A water spider

tir, -a, -e (L). Draw

titan, -o (G My). Gigantic; chalk

tithen (G). A nurse; nursing

tithymal, =us (G). A spurge

titill, -a (L). Tickle

titth, -o, =us (G). A nipple

titub, -a (L). Stagger

titul, =us (L). A title

tityr, =us (G). A pheasant

tla, -s (G). Suffering

=tmema, -to (G). A section, portion

tmesi, =s (G). Separation, division

toc, -o, =us (G). Birth

tod, -i, =us (L). A small bird, a
  tody

=toga (L). A cloak

toich, -o (G). A wall

tok, -o, =us (G). Birth

toler, -a (L). Bear

tolm, -a, -ero (G). Daring, bold

tolyp, =a (G). Wind up; something
  wound up; a ball

tom, =e, -i, -o, =y (G). Cut

toment, -os, =um (L). Dense hair,
  stuffing

ton, -o (G). A tone; tension; something stretched

tons, -or, -ur (L). Shear, cut, shave

tonsill, =a (L). A tonsil

top, -o, =us, =y (G). A place

toph, =us (L). A porous stone

tor, -o, =us (L): Muscle; a swelling;
  (G): a borer

torcul, =a (L). A wine press

=torda (Sw). The razor-billed auk

=toreuma, -to (G). Embossed or
  carved work
toreus, -i (G). Bored through;
  a borer
torfa (LL). Turf
torm, -o, =us (G). A hole, socket
torment (L). A twisted rope; a
  missile; torture
torn, -eu, -o (G). Work with a
  lathe; turn around
toro (L): Muscle; a swelling; (G):
  a borer
torp, -e, -ed, -es, -id, -or (L).
  Numb; numbness; benumb
torqu, -e, -i (L). Twist
torquat (L). Collared
torqui, =s (L). A necklace,
  collar
torr, -e, -i (L). Parch, roast
torren (L). Inflamed, hot; a
  torrent
torrid (L). Dried up, parched
tors, -i, -o (L). Twist
tort, -i (L). Twisted
tortri, -c, =x (L). A tormentor;
  twisted
tortu (L). Winding, twisting
torul, -i, =us (L). A hair tuft
=torus (L). Muscle; a swelling
torv, -i (L). Savage, fierce-eyed
toryn, =a, -i, -o (G). A spoon
tosa (G). Very
tot, -a, -i (L). All
totan, =us (LL). A moor hen
tox, -o, =um (G). A bow
toxic, =um (L). A poison, arrow
  poison
=toxeuma, -to (G). An arrow
trab, -i, =s (L). A beam, timber
trabe, =a (L). A robe of state
trabeculat (NL). Marked with
  cross bars

trach, -i, -y (G). Rough
trache, =a, -i, -o (L). The windpipe
trachel, -o (G). The neck, throat
trachyte (G). Roughness
tract (L). Drawn
trag, -ed, -i (G). Tragedy
trag, -i, -o, =us (G). A goat
=tragopan (L My) A fabulous bird
tram, =a, -o (L). Cross-woven
  fabric, woof
tram, =es, -it (L). A cross way, path
tran, =es, -i (G). Clear, distinct
tran, -s (L). Across, through
transvers, -o (L). Transverse
trapel, -o (G). Easily turned
trapez, =a, -i, -o (G). A table
traphe, -c, =x (G). A spear
trapher, -o (G). Well fed
traul, -o (G). Lisping, twittering
=trauma, -to (G). A wound, shock
travi (L). Penetrate
trech, -o (G). Run, hasten
trechn, -o, =us (G). A branch
=trema, -to (G). A hole
trem, -e, -o, -or, -ul (L).
  Shake, tremble
trep, -o (G). Turn
trepan, -i, -o (G). Bore, bore
  through
treph, -i, -o (G). Feed; thicken
trepid (L). Restless, confused
trepo (G). Turn
trept, -o (G). Turned about, changed
trero, -no (G). Shy
tresi, =s (G). A puncture, hole
tret, -o (G). Perforated
tri (L). Three
tria, -do, =s (G). Three
triaconta (G). Thirty
triaen, =a (G). A trident
trib, -o (G). Rub; a highway
tribel, -o (G). Three-pointed

tribol, -o (G). Three-pronged

tribul, =us (L). Three-pointed; a kind of thorn

trica (L). A trifle

tricesim (L). The thirtieth

trich, -o (G). Hair

tricha, -do, =s (G). A thrush

trichin, -o (G). Hairy; of hair

trichod, -o (G). Hairy

trico (G). Hair

trien, -t (L). One-third

trigesim (L). The thirtieth

triginta (L). Thirty

trigl, =a (G). A mullet

trigon, -o (G). A triangle; triangular

trime, -no (G). Three months

trime, -str (L). Three months

=trimma, -to (G). That which is rubbed

tring, =a (G). A sandpiper

=trio, -no (L). A plow ox

trion, =um (NL). A malvaceous plant

tripan (G). Bore through

tripl, -i, -o (L). Three-fold, triple

trips, -i (G). Friction

tript, -o (G). Rubbed, polished

triquetr (L). Triangular

trism, -o, =us (G). A squeak

triss, -o (G). Triple

trist, -i (L). Sad

trit (L): Rubbed; practiced; (G): the third

tritic, =um (L). Wheat

trito (G). The third

triton (G). A sea god

tritur, -a (L). Rub together, pulverize, grind

trivi (L). Three ways; a crossroads

-trix (L). An agent, or doer of an action

trix (G). Hair; three-fold

troch, -o, =us (G). A wheel

=trochanter (G). A runner; the ball on which the hip bone turns

trochil (G). A pulley; a very small bird

trochle, =a (G). A pulley

trocho (G). A wheel

troct, =es, -o (G). A gnawer; gnawed

trogl, =e, -o (G). A hole, cave

trogo (G). Nibble, gnaw

trom, -o, =us (G). A tremor, trembling

troma, -t (G). Wound

trombid (NL). A little timid one

trop, -ae, -e, -o (G). Turn, change

troph, -i, -o (G). Nourish; food, nourishment

tropi, -d, -do, -o, =s (G). A keel; turn

tropic, -a, -o (G). Tropical

=tropism (G). A turning

tropo (G). Turn, change

=trosis (G). A wounding, an injury

=trox (G). A weevil; a gnawer

truc, -i (L). Fierce

truch, -ero, -o (G). Ragged, worn

truculent (L). Very fierce

trud (L). Thrust, push

trud, -i, =is (L). A pointed pole

trus (L). Thrust, push

=trux (L). Fierce

trunc, -a, -at, =us (L). Cut off, maimed; that which is cut off, the trunk

trutt, =a (LL). A trout

try (L). Three, three times

trybli, -o, =um (G). A cup or bowl

trych, -o (G). Consume

trychin, -o (G). Ragged

trychn, -o, ✻us (G). Nightshade;
  worn out
trygo, -n, -no (L). A dove; a sting
  ray
trym, ✻a, -o (G). A hole
tryp, -a, -ano, -o (G). A hole;
  bore
tryp, -s, -t (G). Rub; rubbed
trypet (G). Bored; a borer
trysi (G). Wearing out
tryss, -o (G). Dainty
✻tsuga (Jap). Hemlock
tub, ✻a (L). A trumpet
tub, -i, ✻us (L). A tube, pipe
tuber, -i (L). A knot, knob,
  swelling
tubercul, ✻um (L). A little knob
  or swelling
tubul, -i, ✻us (L). A little pipe
✻tubus (L). A tube, pipe
tuit (L). Considered; guarded
tulip, -i (F). The tulip
tum, -e, -esc (L). Swell
tumid (L). Swollen
✻tumor, -i (L). A swelling
tumul, ✻us (L). A hill
tund (L). Beat
tunic, ✻a (L). A covering, cloak
tupai (Mal). A tree shrew
tupi, -d, ✻s (G). A hammer
turb, ✻a (L). A crowd, disturb-
  ance
turbell, -a (L). A little crowd
turbid (L). Disturbed
turbin (L). A top; spinning,
  whirling
turbulen, -t (L). Disturbed, confused
turd, -i, ✻us (L). A thrush
turg, -id (L). Swell; swollen
turni, -c, -ci, ✻x (NL). A quail
turp, -i (L). Vile, base

turr, -i, ✻is (L). A tower
tursi, ✻o (L). A porpoise
✻turtur, -i (L). A dove
tuss, -i (L). Cough
tussilag, -in, ✻o (L). The colt's-
  foot
tut, -am, -or (L). Guard, protect
tw, -i, -y (AS). Double
tych, -ae, -e, -ero, -o (G). Chance,
  fortune
tycn, -o (G). Dense
tyl, ✻a, -ar, -o, ✻us (G). A knob,
  knot, pad
tylot, -o (G). Knobbed, knotted
tymb, -o, ✻us (G). A tomb
✻tymma, -to (G). A blow
tympan, -i, -o, ✻um (G). A drum
typ, -i, -o (G). A blow or strike; a
  type
typh, ✻a (G). The cattail
typh, -o, ✻us (G). Smoke
typhl, -o (G). Blind
typi, typo (G). A blow or strike; a
  type
typot, -o (G). Molded
typt, -o (G). Beat, rap
tyr, -eum, -o (G). Cheese
tyrann, -o, ✻us (G). A tyrant, master
tyrb, ✻a (G). Disorder
✻tyto, -n (G). An owl

U

u, -n (L). Not
uber, -i (L). A breast; fruitful
ubiqu, -it (L). Everywhere
ud, -am, -en (G). No one, none
ud, -o (L): Wet; (G): a path, way,
  threshold
ude, -o (G). The ground
udeter, -o (G). Neither
-ul, ✻a, -e, ✻um, ✻us (L). Little
ul, ✻a, -e, -i (G). A scar

ul, -o (G). The gums; curly, woolly; destructive

ulc, -er, =us (L). An ulcer

-ule (L). Little

ule (G). Matter; a scar

=ulex (L). The rosemary

uli, -o (G). A scar; deadly

ulic (L). The rosemary

ulig, -in, =o (L). Moisture

ulm, =us (L). The elm

=ulna (L). The elbow; the ulna

ulo (G). The gums; a scar; curly, woolly; whole; destructive

-ulous (L). Full of

ultim (L). Last, furthermost

ultr, -a, -o (L). Beyond

ultrone (L). Voluntary

ulul, =a (L). Howl, hoot; a screech owl

-ulum; -ulus (L). Little

ulv, =a (L). A sedge

umbell, =a, -i (L). An umbrella

umbilic, =us (L). The navel

=umbo, -n (L). A projecting knob; a shield

umbr, =a, -i (L). Shade

umbros (L). Shady

un (L). Not

un, -a, -i (L). One

unc, -in, =inus, =us (L). A hook

uncia (L). A twelfth; a trifle

uncinat (L). Hooked, with hooks

-uncl, =e (L). Little

unct (L). Anoint; luxurious

-uncul, =a, =um, =us (L). Little

und, =a, -i (L). A wave

undulat (L). Waved, wavy

ungu, =en, -in (L). An ointment

ungui, =s (L). A nail, claw

ungul, =a (L). A hoof

uni (L). One

=unio, -n (L). A pearl

uper (G). Over, above

upo (NL). Under, below

upti, -o (G). Bent backward, inverted

upup, =a, -i (L). A hoopoe

ur (L). Burn

ur, =a, -o (G). The tail

urach, -o, =us (G). The foetal urinary canal

urae, -o (G). The hindmost

urag, -i (G). The rear

urani, -o (G). The heavens; the palate

uranisc, -o, =us (G). The roof of the mouth, palate

urano (G). Heaven

urb, -an, -i, =s (L). A city

urce, -ol, =us (L). A pitcher

ure (G). The tail; urine

ured, -in, =o (L). A blight

ureo (G). Urine; urea

=ureter, -o (G). The ureter

urethr, =a, -o (G). The urethra

urg, =y (G). Work; press

uri (G). The tail; urine

=uria (L): A diving bird; (G): urine

urin, =a, -o (L). Urine; dive

urinator (L). A diver

uro (G). The tail; urine

urs, =a (L). A bear

urtic, =a (L). A nettle

urubu (Br). The black vulture

usne (Ar). Moss

ust, -ici, -ul, -ulat (L). Scorched, browned

ustilag, -in, =o (LL). A smut; a thistle

uter, -i, -o, =us (L). The womb, uterus

util (L). Useful

utri, -c, -cul (L). A leather bag

uv, =a, -i (L). A grape, berry
uvid (L). Damp
uvul, =a, -o (L). The palate .
  uvula
=uxor, -i (L). A wife

V

vac, -a, -u (L). Empty
vacc, =a, -i (L). A cow
vaccin, -i, -o (L). Of a cow; vac-
  cine
vacill, -a (L). Waver
vacu (L). Empty
vad, -o, =um (L). A ford, shallow
  place
vadi (L). Bail, a legal pledge
vag, -a, -an, =us (L). Wandering
vagin, =a, -o (L). A sheath
vagit (L). Crying, squalling
valen, -t (L). Strength; be worth
valerian, =a (L). Valerian
valetud, -in, =o (L). Health
valg (L). Bow-legged
valid (L). Strong
vall (L). A valley; a wall, ram-
  part
vallicul, =a (L). A furrow
valv, =a (L). A folding door; a
  valve
vampyr (Rs). A vampire
van, -i (L). Empty
vanescen (L). Vanishing
vann, -us (L). A fan
vapid (L). Insipid, tasteless,
  spoiled
vapor, -i (L). Steam, vapor
var (L). Bent
varan, -i (Ar). A monitor lizard
vari, -a, -o (L). Change; variegated, mottled
vari, -c, =x (L). A swollen vein
variegat (L). Marked variously

=vas, -a, -o (L). A vessel, duct
vascul, -a, =um (L). A little vessel
vast (L). Laid waste; empty; deso-
  late; huge
vati (L). A prophet; bow-legged
vaticin (L). Prophetic
vect (L). Carried
veget (L). Lively, spirited
vehemen (L). Vigorous, forceful
vehicul, =um (L). A conveyance
vel, -a, -i, =um (L). A veil; a sail
vel, =es, -it (L). A skirmisher
vell, -eri, -os, =us (L). Wool, fleece
vellic, -a (L). Twitch
velo, -ci, =x (L). Swift
=velum (L). A veil; a sail
=velumen (L). Fleece
velutin (NL). Velvety
ven, =a, -o (L). A vein
venat (L). Hunt; hunting
venen, -i, -o, =um (L). Poison
vener, -a (L). Revere, respect
vener, -a, -ea, -i (L My). Pertaining to Venus; coitus, sexual inter-
  course
veni, =a (L). Pardon, favor
veno (L). A vein
venom (L). Poison
vent, -i, -o, =us (L). The wind
vent, =er, -r, -ro (L). The under
  side, belly
vent, -i, -o, =us (L). The wind
ventricul, -o (L). The belly; a
  ventricle
=ventus (L). The wind
=venus (L My). Goddess of love and
  beauty
venust (L). Charming
ver, -a, -ac, -i (L). True; truth
veratr, =um (L). The hellebore
verb, -i, -o, =um (L). A word
verbasc, =um (L). Mullein

verben, =a (L). A sacred herb,
  sacred bough
verd, -an, -i, -ur (OF). Green
veret, -ill, -r (L). The private
  parts, penis
veri (L). True
verm, -i, =is (L). A worm
vern, -a (L). The spring; be
  gay
vernacul (L). Native, local
verricul, =um (L). A net, seine
verruc, =a (L). A wart
vers, -a (L). Turn, change
versi (L). Various; turning;
  verse
versut (L). Shrewd, clever
vert, -a, -e (L). Turn
vertebr, =a, -o (L). A joint; a
  vertebra
vert, =ex, -ic (L). The apex; a
  whirlpool
verticill, -a, =us (L). A whorl
vertig, -in, =o (L). A whirling;
  dizziness
vesan (L). Insane
vesic, =a, -o (L). A bladder
vesicul, =a, -o (L). A little bladder,
  a blister
vesp, =a, -i (L). A wasp
vesper, -i, -tin (L). Evening
=vespertilio, -n (L). A bat
vest, -i, =is (L). Clothing, a coat
vestibul, =um (L). A porch, vestibule
vestig, -i, =ium (L). A footstep,
  trace
vetera, -n (L). Old, of long standing
veterin (L). Of a beast of burden
vetul, =a, -o, =us (L). An old person
vexan (L). Annoying
vexill, =um (L). A standard, banner

=via (L). A way, road
vib, =ex, -ic (L). A whip mark
vibr, -a, -i, -o (L). Shake, vibrate
=vibrissa (L). A hair of the nostrils
viburn, =um (L). The wayfaring
  tree
vicari (L). Substitution, change; a
  substitute
vicen (L). Twenty
=vicia (L). A vetch
vicin, -i (L). Neighboring, near
vict (L). Conquer
victu (L). Food, nourishment
vidu, -i (L). Widowed
viet (L). Shrunken, withered
vigesim (L). The twentieth
vigil, -i (L). Awake, on the watch
vigint, -i (L). Twenty
=vigor, -i (L). Activity, force
vili (L). Vile, base
vill, -i, =us (L). Shaggy hair
villos (L). Hairy
vim, =en, -in (L). A twig, flexible
  shoot
vin, -a, -e, -o, =um (L). Wine
vinace (L). Of wine; wine-colored
vinc (L). Bind, conquer
=vinca (NL). The periwinkle
vincul, =um (L). A confining band
vind, =ex, -ic (L). A claimant; a
  defender
vine, vino (L). Wine
vinnul (L). Delightful
vinos (L). Full of wine
=vinum (L). Wine
viol, -a, -en (L). Injure, profane
=viola, -ce (L). Violet; violet-
  colored
viper, =a, -i (L). A viper, snake
=vipio, -n (L). A small crane
=vir (L). A man
vire, -ns (L). Green

=vireo, -n (L). A kind of bird
virescens (L). Becoming green, greenish
virg, =a (L). A rod; a twig
virg, -in, =o (L). A virgin
virid, -esc (L). Green
viril (L). Manly
viro (L) A poison; a stench
viros (L). Slimy, fetid
virtu (L). Virtue
virul (L). Poisonous
=virus (L). A poison; a stench
=vis (L). Force
vis, -a, -i, -u (L). Look, see
viscer, -a, -o (L). The organs of the body cavity
viscos (L). Sticky
=viscum (L). Birdlime; mistletoe
=viscus (L). An organ in the body cavity
visi (L). Look, see
vit, =a, -al (L). Life
vit, -i, =is (L). A vine; a winding
vitell, -i, -o, =us (L). The yolk of an egg
viti, =um (L). A fault, crime
vitr, -e, -i, -o (L). Glass, glassy
=vitta, -t (L). A stripe, band; striped
vitul, =a, -i (L). A calf
vitupera (L). Find fault with
viv, -a, -i (L). Alive, living
viva, -c, =x (L). Lively, animated
viverr, =a (L). A ferret
voc, -a, -i (L). A voice
vocifer (L). Loud, noisy
vola (L). The palm, sole; fly; the will
volan (L). Flying
voli, -t (L). Wish

volit, -a (L). Fly, fly about
volubil (L). Turning, rolling, fluent
volucr (L). Flying, winged, swift
volum, =en, -in (L). Something rolled up; a volume
volunt (L). The will; a choice
volupt (L). Pleasure
volut, -a (L). Roll, turn
volv (L). Roll, turn
=vomer, -i (L). A plowshare
vomi (L). Discharge, vomit
vor, -a (L). Eat, devour
vora, -c, =x (L). Greedy
vort, =ex, -ic (L). Rotating, whirling; a whirlpool
=vox (L). A voice
vulcan (L My). Fire
vulga, -r, -ri, -t (L). Common, commonplace
vulner (L). Wound
vulp, =es, -i (L). A fox; cunning
vuls (L). Shorn, smooth
vultur (L). A vulture
vulv, =a, -o (L). A covering, wrapper; the vulva

X

xani, -o, =um (G). A comb for wool
xanth, -o (G). Yellow
=xema (NL). A fish-tailed gull
xen, -i, -o, =us (G). A stranger, guest
=xenia (G). Hospitality
xenic, -o (G). Foreign, strange
xenis, =m (G). Entertainment
xeno; =xenus (G). A stranger, guest
xer, -o (G). Dry
xes, -i, -m (G). Polish, scrape; scrapings
xest, -o (G). Polished

xiph, -i, -o, =us (G). A sword
xoan, -o (G). A carved image
xuth, -o (G). Yellowish, tawny
xyel, =a, -o (G). A wood-cutting
  tool
xyl, -o, =um (G). Wood
xyloch, -o, =us (G). A thicket
xylod (G). Woody
xyn, -o (G). Common
xyr, -o, =um (G). A razor
xyri, -d, =s (G). An iris
=xysma, -to (G). Scrapings,
  shavings
xyst, -er, -o, -r (G). Scraped;
  a scraper

Y

y (see also hy)
yl (G). Substance, matter
ymen, -o (G). A membrane
yper (G). Over, above
ypn, -o (G). Sleep
ypo (G). Under, below
yponom (G). Undermine
ypsil, -i, -o (G). Y-shaped
yun, -g, =x (NL). The wryneck

Z

za (G). Very, exceedingly
zabr, -o (G). Gluttonous
zal, =e, -o (G). Sea spray; a
  storm
zamen (G). Forceful, raging
zami, =a, -o (NL). A kind of
  cycad; decayed fir cone
zancl, -o, =um (G). A sickle
ze, =a (G). A grain
ze, -i, =us (G). A kind of fish
zelo (G). Emulate, envy, rival
zem, =a (G). A drink
zemi, =a (G). Loss, damage
zeo (G). Boil, seethe

zephyr, -o, =us (G My). The west
  wind
zeren, -o (G). Dried
zest, -o (G). Boiling; boiled
zete (G). Search for
zeuct, -o (G). Joined
zeug, -o (G). Things paired, a yoke
zeugl, -o (G). The strap of a yoke
=zeugma, -to (G). A band, bond
=zeus (G). A kind of fish; a sea god
zeuxi, =s (G). A joining
zinc, -o (L). Zinc
zingiberi, =s (G). Ginger
ziph, -i, -o, =us (G). A sword
zirco, -n (Ps). Gold-colored
zizani, =um (G). A weed
zizyph, =um (G). The jujube tree
zo, -a, -i, -o, =on (G). An animal
zoarc (G). Maintaining life
zodi (G). A little animal
zodiac (G). Out of animals
zoi (G). An animal
zom, -o, =us (G). Soup, broth; a
  corpulent person
zon, =a, -i (G). A belt, zone,
  girdle
zoo, =n (G). An animal
zoph, -er, -ero, -o (G). Dusky,
  gloomy; darkness
zoro (G). Alive, living, pure,
  strong
zorr, =o (Sp). A fox
zos, -m, -mer, -ter (G). A girdle
zyg, -o, =us (G). A yoke
zygaen, =a (G). The hammer-
  headed shark
zyl, -o (G). Wood
zym, =a, -o (G). Ferment,
  leaven, yeast
zyth, =us (G). A kind of beer
zyxi, =s (NL). A joining

Formulation of Scientific Names

The scientific naming of living organisms follows certain rules which, for animals, are outlined in the International Rules of Zoological Nomenclature, and for plants in the International Rules of Botanical Nomenclature; the basic provisions of these two sets of rules are essentially the same. Scientific names are Latinized, but may be derived from any language or from the names of people or places; most names are derived from Latin or Greek words.

Scientific names are usually descriptive, referring to the size, form, color, habits, or other characteristics of the organism; they are sometimes derived from the names of people or places. The rules permit a name to be merely an arbitrary combination of letters, but such names are not recommended. Names may be Latin or Greek substantives, compound Latin words, compound Greek words, mythological, heroic, or proper names used by the ancients, or Greek or Latin derivatives expressing diminution, comparison, or resemblance. If a modern surname is used to form a scientific name, an ending is added to the name to denote dedication.

Names derived from Greek words should be transliterated according to the rules given below. In compounding two roots to form a name, if the attribute expresses a quality it should precede the principal word (e.g., Erythrocephala); but if it expresses an action, activity, or state it may precede or follow the principal word (e.g., Hydrophilus, Philydrus). When two roots are combined they are usually separated by a combining vowel; the letter i is generally used with Latin roots (although o is sometimes used with second-declension nouns), and o with Greek roots (although y is used with many third-declension nouns). When the second of two combined roots begins with a vowel, the combining vowel is usually omitted. The roots combined to form a scientific name should be from the same source language; exceptions are certain prefixes and suffixes (e.g., anti-, post-, sub-, -oid), which are commonly used with either Latin or Greek roots.

Genus names are formed from modern surnames by adding an ending to denote dedication. Surnames ending in a consonant take the ending -ius, -ia, or -ium (e.g., Williamsonia from Williamson); surnames ending in e, i, o, u, or y take the ending -us, -a, or -um (e.g., Blainvillea from Blainville); surnames ending in a take the ending -ia for

names of animal genera (e.g., <u>Danaia</u> from Dana) or -<u>ea</u> for names
of plant genera (e.g., <u>Jubaea</u> from <u>Juba</u>). If the surname begins with
the particle <u>Mac</u>, <u>Mc</u>, or <u>M'</u> the particle is written <u>Mac</u> and combined
with the rest of the name (e.g., <u>Macneilia</u> from <u>McNeil</u>). If the surname begins with the particle <u>de</u> or <u>von</u>, the particle is either omitted
or coalesced with the name (e.g., <u>Selysius</u> from DeSelys, <u>Delongius</u>
from DeLong). Proper names should not be used with other <u>roots in</u>
the formulation of scientific names.

    Species and subspecies names may be adjectives, the present or
past participles of verbs, or nouns; adjectives and participles must
agree in gender with the genus name, and nouns are either in the
nominative or genitive. Names formed from a modern surname take
a Latin genitive ending: -<u>i</u> if the person is a man, or -<u>ae</u> if the person is a woman; if the surname is that of more than one person (all
having the same surname), it takes -<u>orum</u> if one of the persons is a
man, or -<u>arum</u> if all are women. Particles are handled in the same
way as for generic names (see preceding paragraph). Species and
subspecies names derived from the names of geographic localities
are formed by adding the genitive ending -<u>ae</u> to the locality name, or
by using the adjectival form of the locality name (i.e., with the suffix
-<u>icus</u>, -<u>ica</u>, -<u>icum</u>, -<u>ensis</u>, or -<u>ense</u>, the ending agreeing in gender
with the generic name). Species and subspecies names of animals
always begin with a small letter; species and subspecies names of
plants that are derived from proper names are often capitalized.

    The names of some of the taxonomic categories above genus are
formed by adding the appropriate ending to the root of the name of
the genus that is designated as the type of that group; the endings
that have been standardized are listed below. The names of other
higher categories are Latin plurals in the nominative.

Category	Plants	Animals
Order	-ales	--
Suborder	-ineae	--
Superfamily	--	-oidea
Family	-aceae	-idae
Subfamily	-oideae	-inae
Tribe	-eae	-ini
Subtribe	-inae	--

Anyone formulating a name for a genus of plants or animals should make sure that the name he devises has not already been used. The rules of nomenclature provide that two genera of animals (or plants) cannot have the same name; if it is found that two or more genera have the same name, this name is retained for the first genus for which the name was used, and rejected for the other genera. A genus of plants and a genus of animals can have the same name, although this is not recommended.

In naming species or subspecies, one should make sure that the name he devises is not used for any other species or subspecies in the same genus; otherwise, as in the case of generic names, it would be a homonym and be rejected. It is advisable that the name used be one that is not used in any related genus.

Transliteration of Greek Words

Greek words beginning with a vowel have that vowel marked to indicate the type of breathing used in its pronunciation; a reversed comma above the letter indicates an aspirate (i.e., as though the word began with an h), and a comma above it indicates no aspirate. Words beginning with rho have this letter marked as an aspirate (i.e., with a reversed comma). Transliterations of vowels marked as aspirates have the vowel preceded by h; the transliteration of the letter rho as an initial letter (aspirate) is as rh.

The Greek alphabet consists of 24 letters, as follows:

A	α	alpha	N	ν	nu
B	β	beta	Ξ	ξ	xi
Γ	γ	gamma	O	o	omicron
Δ	δ	delta	Π	π	pi
E	ϵ	epsilon	P	ρ	rho
Z	ζ	zeta	Σ	σ s	sigma
H	η	eta	T	τ	tau
Θ	θ	theta	Υ	υ	upsilon
I	ι	iota	Φ	ϕ	phi
K	κ	kappa	X	χ	chi
Λ	λ	lambda	Ψ	ψ	psi
M	μ	mu	Ω	ω	omega

Greek letters should be transliterated as follows:

ἀ	a		λ	l
ἁ	ha		μ	m
αη	ae (not a diphthong)		ν	n
αι	ai, ae, or e (preferably ae)		ξ	x
αυ	au		ὀ	o (usually short)
β	b		ὁ	ho (usually short)
γ	g		οι	oe, oi, or e (preferably oe)
γγ	ng		final ον	um
γκ	nc		final ος	us
γξ	nx		ου	u or ou (preferably u)
γχ	nch		medial ρ	r
δ	d		initial ῥ	rh
ἐ	e (usually short)		medial ρῥ	rrh
ἑ	he (usually short)		σ	s
ει	ei or i (preferably i)		final ς	s
ευ	eu		τ	t
ζ	z		never initial ὐ	y
ἠ	e (usually long)		initial ὑ	hy
final ἠ	a		φ	ph
θ	th		χ	ch
ἰ	i		ψ	ps
ἱ	hi		ω	o (usually long)
κ	c or k (preferably c)			

Some Common Combining Forms

On the following pages are listed a number of the more common combining forms, or roots, that a taxonomist might use in the formulation of a new name. These roots are listed under a number of categories, as follows:

Colors and Markings
    Basic Colors
    Colors from Metals
    Colors from Other Things
    Qualifying Terms
    Pattern
    Miscellaneous
Size
Shape
Texture
Direction and Position
Numbers
Quantity
Types of Animals
Animal Structures
Common Substances
Types of Plants
Plant Structures
Animal Activities
Habitats
Miscellaneous
Some Common Suffixes

Colors and Markings

Basic Colors

black: (L): atr-, atri-;   (G): melan-, melano-;   (L): nigr-, nigri-
blue: (L): cerule-;   (G): cyano-
bluish gray: (L): caesi-
brown: (L): brunne-;   (L): castane-;   (L): fusc-
gray: (L): glauc-;   (L): grise-;   (G): polio-
green: (G): chloro-;   (L): virid-, viridi-
pale yellow: (L): gilv-;   (G): ochro-
purple: (G): phoenico-;   (G): porphyro-;   (L): purpur-, purpure-
red: (G): erythro-;   (L): rubi-, rubr-, rufi-
reddish orange: (G): pyrrho-
scarlet: (L): coccin-
tawny: (L): fulv-;   (G): cirrho-
violet: (G): ianthin-, iodo-, iono-;   (L): violace-
white: (L): alb-, albi-;   (L): candid-;   (G): leuco-
yellow: (L): flav-;   (L): galb-;   (L): lute-;   (G): thapsino-;
     (G): xantho-

Colors from Metals

bronze: (L): aene-;   (G): chalco-
copper: (G): chalco-;   (L): cupri-
gold: (L): aur-, aurat-, aure-;   (G): chryso-
iron: (L): ferr-, ferro-
lead: (G): molybdo-;   (L): plumb-, plumbe-
silver: (L): argent-;   (G): argyr-, argyro-
steel: (L): chalybd-

Colors from Other Things

ashen: (L): ciner-;   (L): livid-;   (G): tephro-
blood: (G): haemo-, haemato-;   (L): sanguini-
chestnut: (L): castane-
coal: (G): anthraco-;   (L): carb-
flame-colored: (L): flamme-;   (G): pyrrho-
lemon: (G): citrin-, citro-

orange: (L): auranti-;   (G): cirrho-;   (G): croco-
rainbow: (G): irido-
rose: (G): rhodo-;   (L): ros-, rose-
rusty: (L): ferrugin-;   (L): rubigin-
snow: (G): chiono-;   (G): nipho-;   (L): nival-
sooty: (G): aethalo-;   (L): fuligin-;   (L): fumi-
wine: (G): oeno-

Qualifying Terms

dark: (G): amauro-;   (L): calig-, caligin-;   (G): mauro-;
   (L): obscur-
dim: (G): amydro-
dusky: (G): pello-;   (G): phaeo-;   (L): pulli-
pale: (G): ochro-;   (G): liro-;   (L): pallid-, pallidi-

Pattern

banded: (L): fasciat-
checkered: (L): tesselat-
speckled: (G): psaro-
spotted: (G): balio-;   (L): maculat-;   (G): stigmato-
streaked: (L): plagat-
striped: (L): vittat-

Miscellaneous

beautiful: (L): bell-;   (G): calo-;   (L): cypri-;   (L): pulchr-
color: (G): chromato-, chromo;   (L): colori-
glassy: (G): hyalo-;   (L): pellucid-
shining: (G): argo-;   (L): lucid-

Size

dwarf: (G): nano-;   (L): pumili-
equal: (L): equi-;   (G): iso-;   (L): pari-
gigantic: (G): colosso-;   (G): giganto-;   (L): ingenti-;   (G): peloro-;
   (G): titano-
heavy: (G): baro-, bary-;   (L): gravi-
large: (L): grandi-;   (G): macro-;   (L): magni-;   (G): mega-,
   megalo-

largest: (L): maxim-;   (G): megisto-
less than: (G): meio-, mio-;   (L): sub-
light in weight: (G): elaphro-;   (L): levi-
long: (G): dolicho-;   (L): longi-;   (G): meco-
longest: (G): mecisto-
short: (G): brachy-;   (L): brevi-;   (L): curti-
small: (G): baeo-;   (G): micro-;   (L): minut-;   (L): parvi-;
    (G): pauro-;   (L): pusill-
smallest: (G): elachisto-;   (L): minim-
tall: (G): aep-, aepy-;   (L): alti-;   (L): procer-, proceri-
unequal: (G): aniso-

Shape

angled: (L): anguli-;   (G): gonio-
bent: (G): ancylo-;   (G): campto-;   (G): campylo-;   (G): cypho-
blunt: (G): ambly-;   (L): obtus-;   (L): retus-
broad: (see wide)
circular: (see round)
clubbed: (L): clavat-;   (G): rhopalo-
closed: (G): clisto-
coiled: (see spiral)
crescent-shaped: (L): lunuli-;   (G): menisco-
crooked: (G): ancylo-;   (G): rhaebo-;   (G): scolio-
curled: (L): crispi-;   (G): bostrycho-
curved: (G): cyrto-;   (G): gampso-;   (G): toxo-
cylindrical: (L): cylind-, cylindro-
dense: (see thick)
egg-shaped: (L): ovat-
flat: (L): aplanat-;   (L): plani-;   (G): platy-
forked: (G): dicho-;   (G): dicro-;   (L): forficat-;   (L): furc-
form: (L): -form;   (G): morpho-;   (G): schemato-
hollow: (L): alveo-;   (L): cavi-;   (G): coelo-
hooked: (G): ancistr-;   (G): ancylo-;   (G): grypho-;   (L): hamat-;
    (G): onco-
horned: (G): cerato-;   (L): cornut-
lobed: (L): lobat-, lobi-
narrow: (L): angusti-;   (G): steno-

oblique: (see slanting)
open: (L): aperi-; (G): chaeno-; (G): oego-
pointed: (L): acuminat-; (L): muricat-
ragged: (G): carcharo-; (L): pannos-; (G): rhago-
round: (L): circuli-; (G): cyclo-; (G): gyro-; (L): rotundi-;
    (G): strongylo-
shape: (see form)
sharp: (L): acri-; (L): acuti-; (G): oxy-
slanting: (L): declivi-; (G): dochmo-; (G): epiphoro-;
    (G): lechrio-; (G): loxo-; (L): obliqu-; (G): plagio-
slender: (L): gracil-; (G): lepto-; (L): tenui-
sphaerical: (G): sphaero-
spiral: (G): helico-; (L): spirali-; (L): strombi-
split: (G): dicho-; (G): dicrano-; (G): schisto-, schizo-
square: (L): quadrat-
steep: (G): ananto-; (L): ardu-
straight: (G): euthy-; (G): ortho-; (L): recti-
thick: (L): crassi-; (G): hadro-; (G): pachy-; (G): pycno-
torn: (G): rhago-
triangular: (G): delt-; (G): trigono-
twisted: (G): ileo-; (G): plecto-; (G): strepto-; (G): strobilo-,
    strobo-; (G): stropho-
wavy: (L): undulat-
wide: (G): eury-; (L): lati-; (G): platy-

Texture

bare: (G): gymno-; (L): nudi-; (G): psilo-
bearded: (L): barbat-; (L): crinit-; (G): pogono-
downy: (G): pappo-; (L): pubesc-
flexible: (G): campo-
furrowed or grooved: (G): aulaco-; (G): glypho-, glypto-;
    (L): striat-; (L): strigat-; (L): sulcat-
hairy: (G): dasy-; (L): hirsut-; (G): lasio-; (G): trichodo-;
    (L): villos-
hard: (L): duri-; (G): sclero-
keeled: (L): carinat-
network: (G): arcy-; (L): reti-, retin-

punctured: (L): punctat-;   (G): sticto-
rough: (L): asper-, aspr-;   (L): scabr-;   (G): trach-, trachin-,
    tracho-, trachy-
smooth: (G): aphelo-;   (L): glabr-;   (G): leio-;   (G): lisso-;
    (G): lito-
soft: (G): malaco-;   (L): molli-
spiny: (G): acantho-;   (G): echino-;   (L): spini-
woolly: (G): lachno-;   (L): lani-;   (G): mallo-
wrinkled: (L): caperat-;   (L): corrugat-;   (G): rhysso-;
    (L): rugos-

Direction and Position

above: (G): hyper-;   (L): super-, supra-
across: (G): dia-;   (L): trans-
against: (G): anti-;   (L): contra-
apart: (G): dia-;   (L): dis-
apex: (G): acro-;   (L): apic-
around: (L): ambi-;   (L): circum-;   (G): peri-
away: (G): apo-
backward: (G): opisth-, opistho-;   (G): palin-;   (L): retr-,
    retro-
before: (L): ante-, antero-;   (L): pre-;   (G): pro-
behind: (G): opistho-;   (L): post-, postero-
below: (G): hypo-;   (L): infra-
beside: (G): para-
between: (L): inter-;   (G): meta-
beyond: (L): ultra-
crosswise: (G): chaism-;   (L): decussi-
down: (G): cat-, cata-;   (L): de-
eastern: (G): euro-;   (L): oriental-
far: (G): tele-
first: (G): archi-, archo-;   (L): primi-;   (G): protero-, proto-
front: (L): antero-;   (G): proso-;   (G): proto-
inner: (G): endo-, ento-
middle: (L): medi-, medio-;   (G): meso-
near: (G): anchi-;   (G): engy-;   (G): para-;   (L): proxim-
northern: (L): aquiloni-;   (L): arctic-;   (L): boreal-;   (L): septen-
    trional-

opposite: (G): anti-;   (L): contra-;   (G); enanti-
outside: (G): ecto-;   (G): exo-;   (L): extern-
over: (G): hyper-;   (L): super-, supra-
second: (G): deutero-;   (L): secund-
separate: (G): crino-;   (L): divaricat-
side: (L): lateri-, latero-;   (G): pleuro-
slanting: (L): declivi-;   (G): dochmo-;   (G): loxo-;   (G): plagio-
southern: (L): austr-, austral-;   (L): notial-;   (G): noto-
third: (L): terti-;   (G): trito-
top: (G): acro-;   (L): apici-
under: (G): hypo-;   (L): infra-;   (L): sub-
western: (My): hesperi-;   (L): occidental-
within: (G): endo-, ento-;   (L): intra-

Numbers

one-half: (G): hemi-;   (L): semi-
one: (G): mono-;   (L): uni-
one and one-half: (L): sesqui-
two: (L): bi-;   (G): di-;   (L): duo-
double: (G): amphi-, ampho-;   (L): duplici-;   (G): didymo-;
   (G): diplo-
three: (L): tri-;   (G): tria-, triado-
four: (L): quadri-;   (G): tetra-
five: (G): pento-;   (L): quinque-
six: (G): hexa-;   (L): sex-, sexi-
seven: (G): hepta-;   (L): septem-, septen-
eight: (L, G): octo-
nine: (G): ennea-;   (L): novem-
ten: (G): deca-;   (L): decim-
eleven: (G): hendeca-;   (L): undecim-
twelve: (G): dodeca-;   (L): duodecim-
one hundred: (L): centi-;   (G): hecato-
one thousand: (G): kilo-;   (L): milli-

Quantity

all: (L): omni-;   (G): pan-, panto-;   (L): toti-
common: (G): coeno-;   (L): commun-;   (L): vulgar-
equal: (L): equi-;   (G): iso-;   (L): pari-
empty: (G): ceno-;   (L): vacu-;   (L): vani-
even-numbered: (G): artio-
few: (G): oligo-;   (L): pauci-;   (G): pauro-
full: (G): mesto-;   (L): pleni-;   (G): plero-
many: (L): multi-;   (G): myria-;   (G): poly-
more: (G): plio-;   (L): pluri-
most: (G): pleisto-
odd-numbered: (G): perisso-
part: (G): mero-;   (L): parti-
simple: (G): haplo-;   (L): simplici-
single: (G): henico-;   (G): haplo-
solitary: (G): eremit-, eremo-
unequal: (G): aniso-
very: (G): aga-;   (G): ari-;   (G): za-
whole: (G): holo-;   (L): integri-

Types of Animals

animal: (G): zoo-, -zoon
bird: (L): avi-, -avis;   (G): -ornis, ornitho-
cat: (G): aeluro-, -aelurus;   (L): feli-, -felis
caterpillar: (G): -campa, campo-;   (L): -eruca, eruci-
cow: (G): boo-, -bus;   (L): -bos, bov-
dog: (L): cani-, -canis;   (G): cyno-, -cyon
fish: (G): ichthyo-, -ichthys;   (L): pisci-, -piscis
fly: (L): -musca, musci-;   (G): myi-, -myia
frog: (G): batracho-, -batrachus;   (G): -phryna, phryno-;
    (L): -rana, rani-
horse: (L): equi-, -equus;   (G): hippo-, -hippus
insect: (G): entomo-;   (L): insecti-
leech: (G): -bdella, bdello-;   (L): hirudini-, -hirudo
lizard: (L): -lacerta, lacerti-;   (G): sauro-, -saurus

man: (G): anthropo-, -anthropus;   (L): homini-, -homo
mouse: (L): muri-, -mus;   (G): myo-, -mys
pig: (G,: hyo-, -hys;   (L): sui-, -sus
reptile: (G): herpeto-
shellfish: (G): concho-, -concha
snake: (L): aspidi-, -aspis;   (L): -coluber, colubri-;   (G): ophio-, -ophis
spider: (G): -arachna, arachno-;   (L): -aranea, aranei-
turtle: (G): chelono-, -chelys;   (G): emydo-, -emys;   (L): testudini--testudo
worm: (G): -helmins, helmintho-;   (L): vermi-, -vermis

Animal Structures

ankle: (L): tars-, tarsi-, -tarsus
anus: (L): ano-, -anus;   (G): procto-, -proctus
arm: (G): brachi-, -brachium
back: (L): dors-, dorsi-, -dorsum;   (G): noto-, -notus;   (L): terg-, -tergum
bag: (see bladder)
beak: (G): rhyncho-, -rhynchus;   (L): rostr-, -rostrum
belly: (L): -venter, ventr-, ventro-
bladder: (G): asco-, -ascus;   (G): cysto-, -cystis;   (G): -physa, physo-;   (L): -vesica, vesico-
blood: (G): -haema, haemato-, haemo-;   (L): sanguini-, -sanguis
body: (L): corporo-, -corpus;   (G): -soma, somato-
bone: (L): -os, ossi-;   (G): osteo-, -osteum
border: (G): chilo-, -chilus;   (G): craspedo-, -craspedum
brain: (L): cereb-, cerebr-, -cerebrum;   (G): encephalo-, -encephalus
breast: (L): pector-, -pectus;   (L): stern-, sterni-, -sternum;   see also chest
bristle: (G): -chaeta, chaeto-;   (L): -seta, seti-
cartilage: (G): chondro-, -chondrus
cell: (L): -cella, celli-;   (G): cyto-, -cytus
cheek: (L): bucc-, -bucca;   (L): gen-, -gena, geno-
chest: (G): stetho-, -stethus;   see also breast and thorax
claw: (G): chel-, -chela, chelo-;   (G): onycho-, -onyx;   (L): ungui-, -unguis

crest: (L): crist-, -crista; (G): lopho-, -lophus
crown: (L): coron-, -corona; (G): stephano-, -stephanus
digit: (G): dactylo-, -dactylus; (L): digiti-, -digitus
ear: (L): auri-, -auris (L); (G): otido-, oto-, -ous
egg: (G): oo-, -oum; (L): ovi-, -ovum
eye: (L): oculi-, -oculus; (G): -omma, ommato-; (G): ophthalmo-,
    -ophthalmus; (G): opo-, -ops, opto-
eyelash: (G): -blepharis, blepharo-
eyelid: (L): cili-, -cilium
face: (L): faci-, -facies; (G): -ops
feather: (L): -pinna, pinni-; (L): plum-, -pluma, plumi-; (G):
    -pteryla, pterylo-; (G): ptilo-, -ptilum
finger: (see digit)
flesh: (L): carni-, -caro; (G): sarco-, -sarx
foot: (L): pedi-, -pes; (G): podo-, -pus
forehead: -frons, front-; (G): metopo-, -metopus, -metopius
gill: (G): branch-, -branchium, brancho-
gland: (G): -aden, adeno-; (L): glandi-, -glans
groin: -inguen, inguini-
hair: (L): capill-, -capillus; (L): crini-, -crinis; (L): pil-, pili-,
    -pilus; (G): -thrix, tricho-
hand: (G): -chir, chiro-; (L): mani-, manu-, -manus
head: (L): capit-, capiti-, -caput; (G): -cephala, cephalo-
heart: (G): cardi-, -cardia; (L): -cor, cordi-
heel: (L): calcan-, calcane-, -calcaneum; (L): talari-, tali-, -talus
horn: (G): -cera, cerato-; (L): corn-, -cornus
jaw: (G): genyo-, -genys; (G): gnatho-, -gnathus; (L): maxill-,
    -maxilla
joint: (G): arthro-, -arthrum; (L): articuli-, -articulus, -artus
kidney: (G): nephro-, -nephrus; (L): ren-, -ren, reni-
knee: (L): genu-, -genu; (G): gony-, gonyo-, -gonys; (G): -gonatium,
    gonato-
knuckle: (G): condylo-, -condylus
leg: (G): cnemi-, -cnemis; (L): crur-, -crus; (G): -scelis, scelo-
    scelido-
lip: (G): chilo-, -chilus; (L): labi-, labio-, -labium, labr-, -labrum
liver: (G): -hepar, hepato-; (L): jecori-, -jecur
lung: (G): -pneuma, pneumo-; (L): pulmo-, -pulmo, pulmono-

membrane: (G): chorio-, -chorium;   (G): -hymen, hymeno-;   (L):
    membran-, -membrana;   (G): meningo-, -meninx
mouth: (L): ora-, ori-, -os;   (G): -stoma, stomato-
mucus: (G): blenno-, -blennus
muscle: (G): myo-, -mys; see also <u>flesh</u>
neck: (G): -auchen, aucheno-;   (L): cervic-, -cervix;   (L): coll-,
    -collum;   (G): -dera, dero-;   (G): trachelo-, -trachelus
nose: (L): nasi-, -nasus;   (G): rhino-, -rhis
rib: (L): cost-, -costa, costi-;   (G): scelido-, -scelis
rump: (G): gluteo-, -gluteus;   (G): -pyga, pygo-
scale: (G): lepido-, -lepis;   (L): squam-, -squama, squami-
shell: (G): -concha, concho-;   (G): ostraco-, -ostracum
shoulder: (G): omo-, -omus
skin: -byrsa, byrso-;   (G): chorio-, -chorium;   (L): cutan-, cuti-,
    -cutis;   (G): derm-, -derma, dermo-, dermato-;   (G): scyto-,
    -scytus
skull: (G): cranio-, -cranium
snout: (see <u>beak</u>)
sperm: (L): -semen, semin-;   (G): -sperma, spermato-
spine: (G): -acantha, acantho-;   (G): rhachi-, -rhachis;   (L):
    -spina, spini-
stomach: (G): -gaster, gastro-;   (L): -venter, ventr-
suture: (G): -rhapha, rhapho-
tail: (L): caud-, -cauda;   (G): cerco-, -cercus;   (G): -ura, uro-
thigh: (L): femor-, -femur;   (G): mero-, -merus
thorax: (G): thoraco-, -thorax
throat: (L): gula-, -gula;   (L): guttur-, -guttur;   (G): laemo-,
    -laemus;   (G): pharyngo-, -pharynx;   (G): trachelo-, -trachelus
tissue: (G): histo-, -histus;   (L): tel-, -tela, teli-
toe: (see digit)
tongue: (G): -glossa, glosso-, -glotta, glotto-;   (L): -lingu-, -lingua
tooth: (L): -dens, dent-, denti-;   (G): odonto-, -odous, -odus
vein: (G): phlebo-, -phleps;   (L): ven-, -vena, veni-
windpipe: (G): broncho-, -bronchus;   (G): trache-, -trachea
wing: (L): ala-, -ala, ali-;   (G): ptero-, -pterum;   (G): pterygo-,
    -pteryx
wrist: (L): carpo-, -carpus

Common Substances

dust: (G): conio-, -conis; (L): pulveri-, -pulvis
fat: (G): -adeps, adipo-; (G): demo-, -demus; (G): lipo-, -lipus;
    (G): -piar, piaro-; (G): -pimela, pimelo-; (L): sebo-, -sebum;
    (G): -stear, steat-, steato-
flour: (G): aleuro-, -aleurum; (L): farin-, -farina
food: (G): bor-, -bora; (G): -broma, bromato-; (G): sitio-, sito-,
    -situs
glass: (G): hyalo-, -hyalus; (L): vitri-, -vitrum
glue: (G): -colla, collo-; (G): -glia, glio-; (L): -gluten, glutin-
honey: (G): -melis, melito-; (L): -mel, melli-
milk: (G): -gala, galacto-; (L): -lac, lacti-
rock: (L): lapid-, -lapis; (G): litho-, -lithus; (G): -petra, petro-;
    (L): rupi-, -rupis; (L): saxi-, -saxum
salt: (G): halo-, -hals; (L): -sal, sali-, salin-
silk: (L): bombyc-, -bombyx; (L): -ser, seri-, seric-
starch: (G): amylo-, -amylum, -amylus
water: (L): aqua-, -aqua, aquat-; (G): -hydor, -hydra, hydro-
wax: (L): ceri-, -cera; (G): cero-, -cerus
wool: (G): -lachna, lachno-, -lachnus; (G): -mallus, mallo-; (L):
    -lana, lani-

Types of Plants

fern: (G): pterido-, -pteris
fungus: (L): fungi-, -fungus; (G): -myces, myceto-, myco-
grain: (G): -chondrium, chondro-
grass: (L): -gramen, gramini-; (L): grani-, -granum; (G): -poa,
    poo-
moss: (G): bryo-, -bryum; (G): hypno-, -hypnum; (G): mnio-,
    -mnium
plant: (G): phyto-, -phytum
reed: (L): arundi-, -arundo; (G): calamo-, -calamus; (G): donaci-,
    -donax
shrub: (G): thamno-, -thamnus
tree: (L): arbor-, -arbor, arbore-; (G): dendro-, -dendron, -dendrum
vine: (G): ampelo-, -ampelus; (L): viti-, -vitis
wheat: (G): pyro-, -pyrum; (L): tritici-, -triticum

Plant Structures

bark: (L): -cortex, cortici-;   (G): phloeo-, -phloeus
berry: (L): acini-, -acinus;   (G): cocco-, -coccus;   (L): -bacca,
    bacci-
bramble: (G): bato-, -batus
branch: (G): clado-, -cladus;   (L): ram-, rami-, ramo-, -ramus
bud: (L): gemm-, -gemma
flower: (G): -anthemum, antho-, -anthus;   (L): -flora, flori-
fruit: (G): carp-, carpo-, -carpus;   (L): fructi-, -fructus;   (L):
    pomo-, -pomus
leaf: (L): foli-, -folium;   (G): phyllo-, -phyllum
nut: (G): caryo-, -caryum;   (L): nuci-, -nux
root: (L): radici-, -radix;   (G): -rhiza, rhizo-
seed: (G): blasto-, -blastus;   (L): -semen, semini-;   (G): -sperma,
    spermato-;   (G): -spora, sporo-
stalk or stem: (L): cauli-, -caulis;   (G): caulo-, -caulus;   (L):
    petiol-, -petiolus;   (L): -stipes, stipit-
thorn or spine: (G): -acantha, acantho-;   (L): -spina, spini-

Animal Activities

breathe: (G): pneumato-, pneumo-
carry: (L): fer-;   (G): phoro-
creep: (G): erpet-;   (L): rept-, reptili-
cut: (L): sect-;   (G): tom-
dance: (G): choreo-
dwell: (L): col-, coli-;   (G): -ecetes, -etes;   (L): -estr
eat: (G): phago-;   (G): tropho-;   (L): vor-, vora-
fast: (see swift)
feed((see eat)
habit: (G): etho-, -ethus
jump: (L): salt-;   (L): salien-;   (G): scirto-
live: (see dwell)
love: (G): philo-
motion: (G): cine-, cinemato-, cinet-;   (L): moti-
noisy: (L): garrul-;   (G): spharago-;   (G): stombo-;   (L): vocifer-
quick: (G): aeolo-, aeluro-
run: (L): cursor-;   (G): dromo-

sing: (G): acheto-
sleep: (L): dorm-; (G): hypno-; (L): somni-; (L): sopor-
slow: (G): brady-; (L): tardi-
sound: (G): -phona, phono-
swift: (L): celeri-; (L): citi-; (G): tachy-; (L): veloci-
swim: (L): nata-, natant-; (G): necto-; (G): pleo-
turn: (G): trop-, tropi-, tropido-
walk: (L): ambulat-; (G): baeno-; (G): bat-; (L): gressor-
wander: (L): peregrin-; (L): vag-, vagan-

Habitats

abode: (see house)
cave: (L): antro-; (L): caverni-; (G): spel-, speleo-; (G): troglo-
depths: (G): batho-, bathy-; (G): bentho-; (G): bysso-; (G): bytho-
dry: (L): arid-; (G): azo-; (G): xero-
dung: (G): bolito-; (G): copro-; (G): scato-; (G): spatilo-; (L):
    sterco-
dwell: (L): col-, coli-; (G): -ecetes, -etes; (L): -estr
earth: (G): chamae-; (G): chthono-; (G): geo-
field: (L): agri-, agro-; (L): arv-, arvens-; (L): camp-,
    campestr-; (L): prat-, prati-
forest: (see woods)
ground: (see earth)
house: (G): eco-
island: (L): insul-, insular-; (G): neso-
lake: (L): lacustr-; (G): limno-
light: (L): luci-; (G): photo-
live: (see dwell)
marsh: (G): eleo-, elo-; (G): helo-, heleo-, helod-; (G): limno-;
    (L): paludi-
meadow: (see field)
mountain: (L): alpestr-, alpin-; (L): mont-, montan-; (G): oreo-
mud: (G): borboro-; (L): limi-; (L): lut-; (G): pelo-
ocean: (see sea)
place: (G): topo-
pond: (L): stagni-; (G): telmato-
river: (L): amni-; (L): flumini-; (L): fluvia-, fluviatil-; (G):
    potamo-

sand: (G): ammo-; (L): areni-; (G): psammo-
sea: (G): enalio-; (G): halio-; (L): marin-, maritim-; (G): oceano-;
    (G): pelag-, pelago-; (G): thalasso-
shade: (G): scio-; (L): umbri-
shore: (G): aegialo-; (L): litori-
snow: (G): chiono-; (G): nipho-; (L): nival-
swamp: (see marsh)
thicket: (L): dumi-; (G): lochmo-; (G): thamno-; (G): xylocho-
water: (L): aqua-, aquat-; (G): hydro-; (G): hygro-
woods: (G): drymo-; (L): sylvestr-, sylvi-

Miscellaneous

alike: (G): homo-, homoeo-; (L): identi-; (L): simili-; (G):
    tauto-
ancient: (G): archaeo-; (G): palaeo-, palaeonto-
animal: (G): zoo-
different: (G): hetero-; (L): vari-
false: (L): falsi-; (G): pseudo-; (L): spuri-
hidden: (G): aphano-; (G): ceutho-; (G): crypto-
life: (G): bio-
man: (G): andro-; (G): anthropo-; (L): homi-, homini-
moisture: (L): humidi-; (G): hygro-
moon: (L): luni-; (G): menado-, meni-; (G): seleni-
new: (G): caeno-; (G): neo-; (L): novi-
old: (see ancient)
night: (L): noct-, nocti-; (G): nyct-
sun: (G): helio-; (L): sol-
time: (G): chrono-; (L): tempor-
true: (G): eleuthero-; (G): eu-; (L): veri-
visible: (G): delo-; (G): phanero-, phanto-

Some Common Suffixes

-aceae: the ending of names of plant families
-aceus, -acea, -aceum: a Latin suffix meaning "of" or "pertaining to";
    usually used with noun roots
-ago: a botanical suffix denoting resemblance
-ales: the ending of names of plant orders

-alis, -ale: a Latin suffix added to noun roots to form adjectives
     meaning "pertaining to"
-anus, -ana, -anum: a Latin suffix added to noun roots to form adjec-
     tives meaning "belonging to"; often used with names of localities
-atilis, -atile: a Latin adjectival suffix meaning "found in"; usually
     used with roots of nouns referring to habitats
-culus, -cula, -culum: a Latin diminutive suffix
-eae: the ending of names of plant tribes
-ecetes, -etes: a Greek suffix meaning "one who," or "to dwell"; often
     used with roots of nouns referring to habitats
-ellus, -ella, -ellum: a Latin diminutive suffix
-ensis, -ense: a Latin adjectival suffix meaning "belonging to"; usually
     used with locality names
-es: a Greek suffix meaning the doer of an action, used with verb roots;
     equivalent to the English suffixes -er and -or
-escens: a Latin adjectival suffix meaning "becoming," or "beginning
     to"
-estris, -estre: a Latin suffix meaning "belonging to," or "living in";
     generally used with nouns referring to habitats
-etes: (see -ecetes)
-icosus, -icosa, -icosum: a Greek suffix added to verb roots meaning
     "ability," or "fitness"
-idae: the ending of names of animal families
-idius, -idia, -idium: a Latin and Greek diminutive suffix
-iensis, -iense: (see -ensis)
-illus, -illa, -illum: a Latin diminutive suffix
-imus, -ima, -imum: a Latin superlative ending
-inae: the ending of names of animal subfamilies and plant subtribes
-ineae: the ending of names of plant suborders
-inus, -ina, -inum: a Latin suffix denoting "likeness," or "belonging to"
-iscus, -isca, -iscum: a Latin and Greek diminutive suffix
-issimus, -issima, -issimum: a Latin superlative ending
-istus, -ista, -istum: a Greek superlative ending
-odea, -odes: a Greek suffix denoting resemblance
-oidea: the ending of names of animal superfamilies
-oideae: the ending of names of plant subfamilies
-olus, -ola, -olum: a Latin diminutive suffix
-osus, -osa, -osum: a Latin suffix meaning "full of," or "prone to"
-rimus, -rima, -rimum: the Latin superlative ending for adjectives
     ending in er

-tatos: a Greek superlative ending
-ticus, -tica, -ticum: a Latin suffix meaning "belonging to"; generally
    used with roots of nouns referring to habitats
-tus, -ta, -tum: a Latin past participle ending
-ullus, -ulla, -ullum: a Latin diminutive suffix
-ulus, -ula, -ulum: a Latin diminutive suffix
-unculus, -uncula, -unculum: a Latin diminutive suffix